"Having traveled and worked closely with Gayla, I can say that she is passionate about Jesus Christ with all of her heart, soul, and mind. She is a missionary who constantly reaches out to those with whom she comes in contact. She has a gift for communicating the message of God's Word, a passion for sharing it with those who don't know, and making learners of those who do. Her life is a genuine demonstration of active compassion."

—**Iris White,** managing editor of *BaptistLIFE*, Baptist Convention of Maryland/Delaware

"Gayla brings a lifetime of missional living to *Active Compassion: A Calling to Care.* She takes you on a lifelong journey with her missionary stories. Gayla shares great examples of being the feet of Jesus in real-life situations. *Active Compassion* as we go in His name—we all need to do this!"

—**Kaye Miller,** national WMU president, 2005–2010

"*Active Compassion* is a beautiful depiction of kingdom living. Parker is both storyteller and teacher as she challenges us to make a difference in the lives of others. She reminds us of what is most important—know Jesus and make Him known."

—**Tasha Levert,** PhD, conference speaker, worship leader, counselor, and author of *Stories of Hope for the Sleep Deprived*

"John told us that true love is more than words. True love manifests itself in active compassion. Gayla Parker models that active compassion from the missions field in the Philippines to the streets of Baltimore where she lives. Learn active compassion from a practitioner."

—**David Lee,** executive director, Baptist Convention of Maryland/Delaware

"As you read Gayla Parker's new book, you will come to know her heart, soul, and compassion for God's people. She writes with a heart that stirs your emotions, relating to everyday situations that we all experience in one way or another. It will inspire, give insight, and will certainly bless you, as you continue your journey in the Lord."
—**Dr. Jan Bagwell Johnston,** Monroe, Louisiana

"Gayla Parker's passionate relationship with Jesus Christ has made her a difference maker. The pages of this book will draw you closer to Christ as well as compel you to pursue a lifestyle of active compassion."
—**Debbie Smith,** WMU director, Dudley Shoals Baptist Church, and former International Mission Board missionary

"Have you ever seen someone that you thought of as a 'superwoman'? Through the years Gayla has been like a superwoman to me. Gifted in singing, baking, sewing, speaking, teaching, and loving people. The more I grew to know and love Gayla, the more I realized that it was His nature within her that caused her to be her best for His glory. She has a storehouse of experiences, but thrives on people knowing Christ and growing to be more like Him. I would certainly use the word *active* to describe her. There is not a passive bone in her body. How appropriate that she would write about active compassion. Her life embodies this in all she does."
—**SC,** longtime missionary

"Gayla Parker's experiences have prepared her to speak with authority on bringing friends to Christ, even if we have to make a hole in a roof."
—**Andrew Westmoreland,** president, Samford University, Birmingham, Alabama

Active
COMPASSION

Active COMPASSION

A CALLING TO CARE

By: Gayla Parker

NEW HOPE
PUBLISHERS
Birmingham, Alabama

New Hope® Publishers
P. O. Box 12065
Birmingham, AL 35202-2065
www.newhopepublishers.com

New Hope Publishers is a division of WMU®.

Library of Congress Cataloging-in-Publication Data

Parker, Gayla, 1956-
  Active compassion : a calling to care / Gayla Parker.
    p. cm.
  ISBN 978-1-59669-314-2 (sc)
  1. Caring--Religious aspects--Christianity. I. Title.
  BV4647.S9P37 2011
  241'.4--dc23
                          2011033974

ISBN-10: 1-59669-314-2
ISBN-13: 978-1-59669-314-2

N124125 • 1011 • 1.5M1

DEDICATION

To my husband and sons who have filled my life with more blessings than I can count; they are truly amazing men who walk every day with Christ.

To my husband, Freddy, who has loved me unconditionally and who has taught me what it really means to live out our faith while serving others.

To our three sons, Allen, Nathan, and Jesse, who have always been willing to give away their favorite homemade cookies, and give up video game time so the teenagers who swamped our home could play. Our sons amazed me as they adapted to life overseas, and continue to amaze me today as they live out their faith as adult men.

To our three daughters-in law, Christina, Alisha, and Katy. You were prayed for when our boys were born. Thank you for walking alongside our guys, serving our Lord together.

To our mission family in the Philippines who continues to go where no one has gone to take others to the feet of Jesus.

TABLE OF CONTENTS

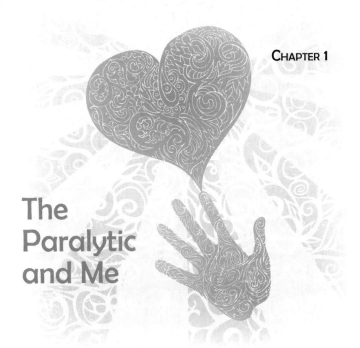

CHAPTER 1

The Paralytic and Me

Walking barefoot in the sand. Waves splashing over feet. Stepping on a stone. New socks. Warm blankets. Things that we enjoy on occasion but more often take for granted were unfamiliar to the paralytic we read about in Mark 2:1–12. He spent much of his life on a floor mat, unable to walk or run or have any sensation of touch in his legs.

We don't know much about this paralytic. We don't know his name, or why his family was not around to help him. We don't know if he was one of many beggars at the city gates every day, or what his life was *really* like. We don't even know why the four men who carried him to the feet of Jesus had active compassion for him.

We do know, however, that his life was changed forever because the four men cared enough for him and had faith enough in the healing power of Jesus to take action. These men not only had compassion for someone who was pitiful, they acted on that compassion. When we put action with our compassion, we have *active compassion*. Sometimes we are the giver of active compassion, and other times we are the recipient of active compassion. But either way, there is nothing quite like it!

There was a difficult time in my life when I was the recipient of active compassion, and it changed me forever. In the fall of 1994, for six weeks of my life, I learned what it was like to be paralyzed. During those weeks, no one was sure if my condition would be permanent or temporary. I learned a lot about myself, my family, my God, my faith, and active compassion.

My husband and I were missionaries in the southernmost island in the Philippines, serving in General Santos City. We loved the city and the Filipinos who served alongside us in our ministry. As far as we were concerned, we would live there until retirement. Just when we were comfortable—our house was in order with all the rooms' decor to my liking and the last picture had been hung; our boys were doing well; and life was going smoothly—everything changed. Isn't it funny how it always seems to work out that way? I'm almost afraid to hang the last picture these days because it seems that is when God brings about a change.

One September morning, I woke up with extreme back pain. My first thought was *a hot shower would help*. My next memory is being on the floor in the shower, unable to get up. A disk in my back had ruptured, a minor injury by today's standards.

I was paralyzed because the swelling had pinched my spinal cord in half like pinching a drinking straw. On that morning, we had no idea what had happened. General Santos has no ambulance service, so my husband carried me to our car and drove me to the hospital. The only piece of equipment there was an x-ray machine. The doctor thought that my back was broken, but the x-ray did not confirm his diagnosis. His next thought was a ruptured disk, but that did not explain the paralysis. For the next two weeks, I stayed in my bed at home, battling intense pain with anti-inflammatory medications, and hoping that whatever was wrong would correct itself.

During those early weeks, the pain did not allow for much sleep, so I decided to bury myself in God's Word. That's when I looked on the story of the paralytic with new eyes. Suddenly, I realized the frustration he must have felt every day with no hope of anything better. I realized how humiliated he must have felt on occasion. I realized the huge impact that the active compassion of four men had on his life. And I imagined what it would have been like to be healed. Were it not for the four men, the paralytic might not have been healed.

Today, there are 6 billion people who have never heard the name Jesus. They may not be physically paralyzed, but they are certainly spiritually paralyzed. They are living with the frustration of life without the grace of God. They are living without hope. We can make a difference simply by living lives of active compassion.

BE PRESENT

The four men were present for the paralytic. Just being there can sometimes be enough. As we traveled into remote villages, we heard over and over again, "No one has ever come here to be with us." Just our presence was a strong enough witness to stir their interest in hearing about Jesus.

My son, Nathan, reminded me during the early days of my injury how important just being there is. Sometimes he sat quietly for hours in my room instead of going outside to play with his friends. He said, "I just want to be with you, Mom. We can talk if you want." He was expressing active compassion.

During those hours, I began to wonder how many talks with my sons had I missed because I was picking up clutter, making beds, or mopping up footprints? How many talks with God had I missed because of my busyness? How many opportunities of simply being present had I missed because of my "to-do" list?

Nathan ministered to me in a way he will never know when he sat with me. He gave me the chance to reevaluate my own life. So often we place our value on all that we do, instead of who we are in Christ. It is not a long "to-do" list that determines our value. What a blessing it is to know that who we are in Christ is enough!

There are people just waiting for someone to be present in their life. Hospital patients, nursing home residents, homeless, unreached people groups around the world, pregnant teens, urban poor, rural poor, victims of violent acts, victims of natural disasters, parents with terminally ill children, children with terminally ill parents, victims of human exploitation, the mentally ill, the parents of autistic children, children of addict parents, parents of addict children, prostitutes, widows, widowers, the stock broker that lost it all, the Muslim, the Buddhist, the Mormon, the atheist—the list of people all in need of a follower of Jesus to be present in their lives is endless.

Just being present may be an easy thing to do, but it may well be one of the most important things we do as believers. It is the first introduction of Jesus. It is the encouragement that can get a believer through their most difficult trial. We may not know all the right words to say, but that is OK, because simply being there is more than sufficient. Just being present through someone's difficult situation is active compassion.

Nathan sitting with me all afternoon is an unforgettable moment in my life. Our presence may be that unforgettable moment in the life of someone searching for hope.

Just as I enjoyed Nathan's presence, Jesus enjoys those times with us when we are in His presence. He loves when we simply sit with Him. To be truly present with others, we should first take time to be present with Jesus—a lesson Martha had to learn many times over.

In Luke 10:38–42, we read about a woman who learned that being in the presence of Jesus is enough. Martha, like so many of us, was all about getting everything done on the "to-do" list. Jesus wasn't primarily interested in her busyness; He was interested in their time together.

In John 11, Martha was the one running out to meet Jesus and complaining to Him about her brother's death. In John 12, she is serving dinner, being busy and "useful" when Mary comes in and pours perfume on the feet of Jesus as an act of worship. All three instances are reminders to Martha of the importance of just being with Jesus.

Granted, leaving the laundry for an indefinite period of time is never a good idea. However, leaving it for another day to spend time with our Lord, a family member, a child, a friend, a patient, can be a life-changing experience.

Jesus said to Martha, "Martha, Martha . . . you are worried and upset about many things, but only one thing is needed." So often we are upset about many things when our focus should be on the One—Jesus. When our focus is on Jesus, then active compassion becomes an extension of Him.

💜 Read Luke 10:38–42; John 11:17–44; and John 12:1–8.

💜 What lessons can you learn from the lives of Mary and Martha?

💜 What are the busy things you can let go of in order to spend time with Jesus?

💜 What are the busy things you can let go of in order to spend time with others?

Making a difference requires being present in the lives of others. Spending time with our children, family members, friends, or those in need requires a conscious choice. Decide now what your plan will be to make it happen and write it down.

There is space in the back of this book to journal.

BE A FRIEND

The friendship the four men had with the paralytic made an eternal difference. They are not alone in the category of friends who make a difference. David and Jonathan in the Old Testament had a unique friendship. Jonathan came to the aid of David when he was in danger. Only a trusted friend could be that bold! Perhaps it was his active compassion for David that gave him the boldness to say the hard things David needed to hear.

A former Muslim once told me about saying the hard thing to his family—"Jesus is the only way to heaven." Their reaction was harsh. He was shot in the side by one family member. Another family member cut his throat with a knife. And another hit his head repeatedly with a rock. He had all the scars to prove his experience. But he said something I will never forget, "I would rather tell them the truth in love than keep silent in fear. Telling them the truth may lead to more beatings or even death, but my eternity is secure. My silence may be less dangerous for me, but it will be deadly for them because my silence will ensure their eternity in hell. So, I will keep loving them by telling them the truth." What an example of what it means to truly be a friend!

Mary and Elizabeth in the New Testament had a very special bond. Both women were expecting babies who would change the world. But the circumstances of their pregnancies were vastly different. Elizabeth was old for childbearing, but she was at least happily married. Mary, on the other hand, was very young and not yet married. Just imagine how difficult it must have been for Mary to tell her cousin that (by proper, modern, western standards) she was virgin who was expecting. Who would believe such a thing?! There must have been an incredible level of trust between these two women. Their time together in those early months of pregnancy must have felt like a wonderful gift from God. Elizabeth's encouragement and acceptance of Mary was active compassion at work.

Throughout the weeks of my paralysis, many friends were there making a difference in my life and in the lives of those who were watching. Two weeks after my back injury, I was still not walking. The decision was made to transfer me to a larger city with better medical care. We found out that the local airlines would not transport a patient. Plan B was a call to a New Tribes missionary pilot, Martin Burnham, whom I had never met. Martin would fly from Malaybalay to General Santos, and then fly me from General Santos to Davao City. Martin's plane was not large enough to carry our entire family, so my husband and three boys traveled by car. Suzie, a missionary friend who lived in Malaybalay, heard about the plans and made the decision to join Martin on his flight so that I would not be making the trip alone. What a wonderful expression of active compassion that turned out to be!

Suzie was expecting her fifth child. When she arrived at the makeshift runway, Martin was herding cattle off the field. Before he could get to his plane, the cattle would be back in the middle of the run-way. Only on the missions field do you encounter these problems! Suzie took over cattle duty and ran the cattle off the runway while Martin started the engines on the plane. It took many tries in the heat to accomplish the task, but at last the cattle were off the field; Martin had the plane started; Suzie was on board; and they were taking off, headed to General Santos. I had no idea she was coming, but I wept when I saw her on the plane and laughed when I heard about the cattle. Her active compassion had already reminded me of God's provision of friends.

Suzie was not the only friend who came to my aid that day. When the plane landed in General Santos, I was not the only one waiting at the airport. The Filipino pastors who worked alongside us were there. Many of them had walked for four to six hours to get there. It was their active compassion that drove them to make that hike and take me to the feet of Jesus through their prayers. They had prayed for many years that God would send them a missionary. God answered their prayers by sending the Parker family. Now it appeared God was taking their missionary away. If God had answered their prayers by sending us to General Santos, then surely He would answer their prayers and bring us back. Before the plane left the General Santos airport that day, the pastors gath-ered around the plane and prayed for God's healing, protection, and deliverance back to our home. I may have been the missionary, but the national pastors were the real heroes.

Martin had taken all but two seats out of his plane. He placed a mattress on the floor of the plane where I laid on the journey to Davao. Moving me from our truck to the mattress on his plane was painful, but it had to be done. The whole ordeal was an emotional and stressful time. Martin seemed to know that it was time for a little humor. Flying is not my favorite thing, but that day I laughed through the entire flight. I even laughed when he suggested that he fly upside down so that I could enjoy the beautiful view. Really, I could have done without seeing the view! His humor was active compassion.

In Davao, friends were present. You think hospital food in America is bad! In the Philippines, breakfast is rice and the head of the fish. Lunch is rice and the middle of the fish. Supper is rice and the tail of the fish. Ben and Pam came to the rescue with homemade pizza for supper. Not only did they feed me daily, but they kept my children for two weeks. Glen and Marvella were taking care of insurance issues. Stan prayed over me every day. Susan brought me books to read. Linda, our nurse, checked my charts with every visit. Shirley found Dr Pepper for me—nothing short of a miracle! My youngest slept under my hospital bed so he would be close. My husband slept every night in a hospital chair by my bed.

Friends whom I knew intimately and friends I knew casually were there. What my friends did for me in the Philippines can be done every day in whatever city we live in—praying, caring, meeting needs, laughing, and crying.

Have you ever wondered why so many people spend time in neighborhood pubs and bars? My guess is they are looking for friends with active compassion. As believers, we can fill that gap. Is there someone you see on a daily basis in need of a friend? Could it be that such a person will meet Jesus through your friendship?

Acceptance is sometimes what true friendship is about. Just to clarify, I'm not talking about the acceptance of sin, but the acceptance of the person. Betty is a volunteer who works with HIV/AIDS patients. In spite of their illness and lifestyle, Betty offers her friendship and concern. It is through her acceptance and love that many have found a relationship with Jesus Christ and found the courage to change their lifestyle.

❤ Read the story of Jonathan and David in 1 Samuel 19–20. List the characteristics of a good friend found in their story.

❤ Read the story of Mary and Elizabeth in Luke 1:39–56. Why do you think Mary had such confidence in her friendship with Elizabeth? How had the Holy Spirit prepared Elizabeth for Mary's visit?

❤ What can you learn about your own friendship and the kind of friend you are through their stories? What are the ways you express active compassion in those relationships?

REFLECTIONS

Four weeks into the paralysis, I was once again moved to a larger hospital in a larger city. Two weeks later, it was clear that I would be leaving the Philippines for the United States on a stretcher.

There was nothing that was easy during those six weeks. But I would not trade a single day for the lessons I learned about God, His love, His provision, His deliverance, and the importance of active compassion. My experience with paralysis was brief in comparison with the paralytic in the Book of Mark. I wonder if, like me, he would not trade a single day because of the miracle he experienced as a result of his paralysis. If he had not been paralyzed, he would not have been taken to the feet of Jesus. Perhaps he might not have met Jesus at all. This hard thing in his life was the very thing that brought him great joy on the day of healing. Like me, he learned about God, His love, His healing power, His grace, His provision, and His deliverance.

As for me, the day after our arrival in the United States, I was in surgery with a very gifted and talented neurosurgeon. When I woke in the recovery room, the surgeon, nurses, and anesthesiologist were all there waiting with anticipation to see if my legs had regained any feeling. It was an exciting moment when indeed my legs were working. The surgeon thinks I was healed because of his exceptional skills. But I know the truth. While he was good, God is great!

For sure, there is not much we know about the paralytic in the Book of Mark. But after my six weeks with paralysis, I understand better the sheer joy he must have felt when he was healed. What if his friends had not had active compassion? What if they had not carried him to the feet of Jesus? He never would have known what it was like to be in the presence of Jesus. He never would have known the blessing of friends. He never would have known the joy of being healed both physically and spiritually. The crowd would not have seen a miracle. Mark 2:12 says, "This amazed everyone and they praised God, saying, 'We have never seen anything like this!'" Multiple lives changed, bringing praise to God, because a few had active compassion for a friend.

💜 What do you think life would have been like for the paralytic we read about in Mark 2:1–12? (no wheelchairs, embarrassment to his family, etc.) Do you pass by people every day that may be living life with similar challenges? Have you taken time to be their friend?

💜 Why was his healing so amazing? (perhaps he was considered not worthy of healing, this was the first time the crowd saw Jesus, etc.)

💜 What event or circumstance in your own life has led you to feeling amazed by the acts of God through that experience?

❤ List all the ways that God proved faithful in your circumstance. Keep the list nearby as a reminder of the power of God.

ACTS OF COMPASSION

💜 Contact the children's floor of your local hospital and offer to volunteer a few hours a week to read to children, clean the playroom, bring reading material to parents, or perhaps snacks for the staff.

💜 Nursing homes are often under staffed and have residents who have few or no visitors. A few hours a week just sitting and reading the local newspaper to a resident or listening to a little music with a patient can turn a hard day into a wonderful day.

💜 There may be any number of reasons a person is paralytic. Regardless of the reason, the needs are the same. Rehabilitation Centers, Handicap Olympics Program, and schools with disabled children have a long list of needs for volunteers. Call and ask how you can be a part and begin making a difference.

💜 When you see a car with a handicap tag or pass a paralytic in the store, take a few minutes to breathe a prayer for that person and their family.

CHAPTER 2

Caring for Others

In the story of the paralytic, we are not told the names of the four men who carried their friend. We do not know if they were longtime friends or if they had ever shown an interest in him before this day. But there are some things we can learn about them as we read their story. We know that they cared. Only someone who cared would go to such great lengths. They cared enough to commit to carrying him across town and adjusting their plans once they arrived. The fact that they even thought to carry him to Jesus is evidence of their concern. The man was in their thoughts; they cared about his future; and they decided to do something about it. If the paralytic wondered if anyone cared about him, he now had his answer.

How many times a week do the people around us feel no one really cares? The list would be miles long.

I heard a gang member say he would never enter a church because no one in there cared about him. His answer is all too common.

Between long "to-do" lists, children, work, spouses, household needs, parents, pets, and more, the day can seem overwhelming. "Mom, can you..." "Honey, can you..." "The boss needs you to..." "The house needs to be cleaned..." "The dog needs to go out..." "Parents need you to...." "The yard needs mowing..." "The oil in the car needs changing..." "The porch needs painting..." "There is absolutely nothing in the house to eat..." "Everyone is on their last set of clothes..." "No washer in the world is big enough for the pile..." Well, you get the idea. While we enjoy family life, the demands can sometimes cause us to feel like a working robot rather than a person who is loved, cared about, and cherished.

The paralytic probably felt neglected and unloved. Was there anyone to ask him how his day had been? Who cared about his meals? Did anyone help him bathe? Perhaps the only signs of compassion came from coins thrown at him. What did he think when the four men came along with their active compassion, offering to take him to Jesus? Knowing that someone had noticed him had to be overwhelming. Even more, the men saw him as a person with a need.

Every day, all of us have needs in various shapes, forms, and degrees. At times, we need friends to come along with active compassion. Sometimes the need is big, sometimes the need is small, and sometimes we aren't even sure we have a need.

The paralytic had a huge need. Most people we know will never face that kind of need, but even meeting little needs speaks volumes.

Sending my first-born to kindergarten was difficult for me. He was excited, but I was apprehensive. On that first day of school, a thousand questions were going through my mind. Would his teacher show him kindness? Would he be afraid all day? Who would hug him when he fell? Would he be able to find his way around the school?

My friend Nancy knew this would be a hard day for me. She cared. She baked a pie, purchased a soda, and spent the entire morning with me. It was a simple act of kindness that encouraged a young pastor's wife. To this day, when I make Nancy's pie, I smile and take a quick inventory of my own life to be sure I'm not neglecting the little acts of compassion and care that can change a day from bad to good.

❤ What day-to-day circumstances might someone you know be facing today? How could you help?

TAKING AN INTEREST

Jesus was the Master of showing an interest in others, taking care of the little things (along with the big things), and showing genuine concern. We don't have to search long to find His story of active compassion. In the Book of Mark, chapter after chapter is packed full of miracles, stories, and parables that show us the compassionate heart and acts of Jesus.

In Mark chapter 10, we read about Jesus and a large crowd of followers entering the city of Jericho. A blind man named Bartimaeus was sitting by the roadside begging. A blind beggar right outside the city gates on a road travelers followed on the way to Jerusalem was a common sight. Most likely, people walked by the beggars, paying little or no attention to them. On this particular day, Bartimaeus calls out, "Jesus, Son of David, have mercy on me!" Some people ignored him, others rebuked him, but Jesus stopped and called for Bartimaeus. At that moment Bartimaeus had a choice to make: he could draw closer to Jesus and accept His active compassion or he could stay where he was, lying on the ground by the city gate.

Even though the story of Bartimaeus took place long ago, Jesus calls out to us today, asking us to make decisions. His first call is inviting us into a saving relationship with Him. It is hard for me to imagine Bartimaeus refusing to go before Jesus when he knew that Jesus could restore his sight. The "for" list would far outweigh the "against" list in that situation. Even in today's skeptical society, if someone could be miraculously healed, they would readily accept the offer. So why is it that so many people today have such a hard time saying yes to His active compassion of spiritual healing?

Perhaps we can find some answers in the passage before the account of Bartimaeus, in the story of the rich young man. In Mark 10:17–31, we read about Jesus meeting a wealthy young man who wanted to know what he must do to inherit eternal life. Jesus responded by reminding the young man about the

Ten Commandments. The young man argued, "I have kept these since I was a young boy." Even though he had followed the Commandments, he instinctively knew there was something missing.

God created us to be in fellowship with Him, and when we are not, our instincts tell us something is not quite right. God wants us to be in fellowship so much that His active compassion included sending His Son, Jesus, to the Cross.

The next verse is such a tender moment in Scripture; Jesus looked at the young man and loved him. Even in the rich man's struggle, Jesus still loved this young man. Even in His rejection, Jesus still loved this young man. Because of this love, Jesus tells him he is indeed lacking one thing: the willingness to let go in faith of what he owns to follow Him. For the rich young man, his first expression of active compassion would mean letting go of his riches. Jesus was asking the rich young man to have faith in God's provision.

For this rich young man, a life of good works was easier than a life lived by faith—as it is today. Just living an honest life, being kind to other people, giving to the poor, being loyal to our spouse, and not committing murder isn't enough. Jesus wants us to be in relationship with Him. It is the difference between looking at a picture of someone or actually being in their presence!

The Ten Commandments gives us a picture of what is good; but it is more blessed to be in the presence of the very One who *is* good! I have no doubt that if this young man had sold all of his possessions, he would have been blessed beyond measure in his relationship with Christ. He would have been blessed through the lives that would have been touched. He would have been blessed to know what it is to have God supply every need. He would have been blessed for eternity instead of being blessed in the temporary. He would have known the wealth of Jesus Christ! His willingness to surrender all and live a life of obedience to Christ would have changed his life from one of good deeds to one of living active compassion.

That first call to join Jesus in a relationship requires that we be willing to come to the place of complete surrender. We are required to surrender our desires, our time, our prestige, our reputation, our health, our spouse, our children, our parents, our home, our education, our all. Not because Jesus wants to take it away from us, but because He wants to bless us in it! He wants to give us blessings that will last longer than our lifetimes—they will last for all eternity. That is only a small part of His active compassion.

Hebrews 11 tells about men from the Old Testament who were willing to follow God in complete surrender. It was by faith they could step out in such total obedience. The writer of Hebrews describes faith like this: "Now faith is being sure of what we hope for and certain of what we do not see" (Hebrews 11:1).

❤ Read Hebrews 11.

❤ List each of the men and women who acted out of faith. What was their act of obedience?

❤ What was the reward for their acts of surrender?

💜 Is it possible to please God without faith?

💜 Is it possible to give complete surrender to God without faith?

💜 How's your faith today?

YES VERSUS NO

Mark 10:22 reveals a sad picture of the rich young man and many people who have come after him who could not give up their possessions for the call of Christ. Scripture says even his countenance cried out sadness: "the man's face fell." He realized that he was giving up an eternity in paradise for a temporary life of wealth. He could follow the Commandments, but he did not have the faith. If only he could have held on to what Jesus later says to His disciples: "With man this is impossible, but not with God; all things are possible with God." In his own power, it was impossible for this man to give up all of his wealth. Only because of the power of God can we relinquish all of our possessions and, in faith, follow Christ.

When God calls us, we must take that first step of surrender, but after that, God takes over and guides every single step that follows. What a wonderful blessing to know that the God who promised in Jeremiah 29:11, "I know the plans I have for you, plans to prosper you and not to harm you,...plans to give you hope and a future" is the same God that takes care of the most precious things in my life. Because I know His plans for me are good and that

He is good, I can hand it all over to Him, knowing it is in the best hands of all, the hands of the very God who created it all and loved it all enough to send His Son to the Cross. When I let earthly things go, then God can work through me as I live a life of active compassion.

Once we say yes to His call of salvation, we will make decisions every day to continue walking closer and closer to Him. Even Jesus, during His life on earth, chose to follow the will of His Father every day. When He faced the 40 days in the desert and was tempted by everything Satan could throw at Him, He chose to continue to be obedient to His Father. When He went to the Cross, He chose to be obedient to His Father. Remember how He cried out to God, "If it is possible, may this cup be taken from me"? The cup could not be taken away; it was still the will of the Father for Him to bear the Cross for us, you and me, that we might have salvation. For six hours, Jesus hung on the Cross and was beaten beyond recognition because He chose to follow the will of the Father. His obedience was being lived out in His active compassion for the lost.

Jesus' walk of obedience was unique; it required that He leave heaven, become as man knowing every temptation that we know when He had been without temptation, and He had to walk the road to the Cross. This side of heaven, I will never know life without temptation. But it is my desire that my heart will be so obedient to the will of Christ that it will no longer be recognizable as mine, but instead it will look like my Lord. It will be a heart full of compassion, mercy, patience, kindness, joy, peace, love, and all the rest! The fullness of all that is in my heart will spill over to active compassion so that others might experience the love of Christ. Every single day, I have to make that choice. Every day, I choose if I will say like Joshua, "As for me . . . I will serve the Lord" (Joshua 24:14–15).

There are many who have decided to choose Christ. Bartimaeus is only one of many. He chose that day at the city gate to get up—actually the passage says he jumped up—and go to Jesus. What a wonderful act of enthusiasm! Not only was he willing to come to Jesus, but he jumped up in excitement at the very thought of coming to Jesus. Oh, that we would all come to Jesus every day with that kind of enthusiasm!

Jesus asked, "What do you want me to do?" Bartimaeus answered, "I want to see." For Bartimaeus, he was referring to his physical sight. But there is much to learn from his request. Our hearts cannot be changed unless we are willing to perceive the things that need to be changed. We may remain unaware of others' needs until God enlightens us.

When our youngest son, Jesse, had chicken pox, he wanted to keep his clothes on 24/7. At the time, we were living in the Philippines in a very hot and humid climate. All of us were puzzled by his insistence on staying fully clothed. When I finally asked why, he answered, "Chicken pox are ugly, and I don't want to see them!"

As Christians, many of us don't want to acknowledge the sin that is in our hearts and in our world. We want to cover it up rather than to expose it to Christ for His healing. The effect of sin is ugly and all around us—poverty, AIDS, immorality, violence, and all the rest. Only when we acknowledge it can we begin the process of change.

Active compassion involves acknowledging, too, the sin that prevents *us* from being obedient. Recognizing the work of the Holy Spirit around us and joining with Him in that work. Seeing the hurt around us so that we can have active compassion.

"Go," said Jesus, "your faith has healed you." Bartimaeus could immediately see, and he followed Jesus along the road. This man who may have never seen the blue sky, the bright sun, the dusty road, the people that came through the city gate, the face of the Savior, could now see everything. This was not a small moment in his life; this was *huge*! His next step was to follow Jesus along the road.

That is our next step too. Once we can see, it is time to follow the example Jesus set before us and live a life of active compassion.

♥ Read Mark 10:13–31, 46–52.

♥ What are the expressions of active compassion we see in the life of Jesus in these verses?

♥ What can we learn about living our day-to-day lives with active compassion from these verses?

In Mark 10:51 we read, "'What do you want me to do for you?' Jesus asked him. The blind man said, 'Rabbi, I want to see.'"

❤ Pray and ask Jesus to help you perceive your neighborhood, workplace, family, and friends in a new way. Pray that you will recognize the needs that are around you every day. Pray for ways to meet those needs as you live a life of active compassion.

In Mark 10:52 we read, "He [Bartimaeus] received his sight and followed Jesus along the road." Each one follows Jesus in a unique way. How is He calling you to follow Him?

IT'S THE LITTLE THINGS

Have you ever noticed how the big trials of life take us to our knees, but the day-to-day hassles of life can drive us crazy? Perhaps in the daily grind we feel the most alone. But Jesus cares even about the little things! The psalmist in 68:19 sings out in praise, "Praise be to the Lord, to God our Savior, who daily bears our burdens." Imagine that! He *daily* bears our burdens. God is not only interested in the big rescue moments, He is there every day ready to carry the weight of multi-tasking, family, work, bills, teenagers, school, even the laundry.

The most romantic moments in my marriage are not always the roses and chocolates, but coming home to a clean house or all the laundry done or the homework already done. Why does that carry such an impact? Because someone cared about the little day-to-day stresses. As nice as that is, now consider the magnitude of Psalm 68:19—God Himself daily bears our burdens.

Jesus reminds us again in Luke 12:22–34 that God will always be there to take care of every need. We can look around us every day and see the evidence in our world; the birds are fed and clothed. Verse 32 says, "Do not be afraid, little flock, for your Father has been pleased to give you the kingdom." The reality of that is *huge*. God is pleased to give us the kingdom. The entire kingdom is ours when we are His. There is no fear in living out active compassion, because God is already there.

♥ Find two other passages of Scripture that indicate God cares about the little things in our lives. Write them down and read them every day as a reminder of God's daily presence.

♥ How many miracles and teachings of Jesus can you find that are about the "little" things?

♥ What does that teach us about how and when we should pray?

♥ What are the "little" things in your life that you need to give to Jesus so that He can daily bear your burden?

♥ How can you be a part of God's provision for someone you know?

♥ Pray and ask God to reveal Himself to others through the little things that you do for others every day.

CARING

"You just don't care!" is said by teenagers all over the world every day. Even David cried out to God in Psalm 10:1, "Why, O LORD, do you stand far off? Why do you hide yourself in times trouble?" Retranslated: "Don't you care?!"

In John chapter 11, we hear the cry of a sister who questioned if Jesus really cared. "Jesus, where is your active compassion today when I need you?!" Martha's brother, Lazarus, was very ill. Martha and her sister, Mary, sent word to Jesus that Lazarus was about to die. Their hope was that Jesus would come quickly and heal their brother. Jesus loved Mary and Martha. Yet when He got the message, He stayed where He was for two more days. Imagine how frustrated these sisters must have been! If Jesus loved them so much, why was He delaying His return to their home? Lazarus is dead. *If Jesus really cared, He would not have allowed our brother to die.* All these thoughts and more must have been going through their hearts.

When Jesus finally arrived at the house, Lazarus had been in the tomb for four days. Martha went running out to meet Jesus on the road, crying, "Lord,... if you had been here, my brother would not have died." Even though Jesus assured her that Lazarus would rise again, Martha assumed He was referring to the final resurrection. Jesus had to be thinking, *Martha, listen to me; my dear, sweet child, stop fretting. I'm here to take care of this, and your brother will be with you today. You do not have to wait for the resurrection of the saints.*

It is easy to look back on this conversation and wonder how Martha could be arguing the point with

Jesus, but in reality, we all do it every single day. "But, Jesus, wouldn't it be better if . . . ." "I have a good idea on this one, Lord." We like to know the plan (when, how, and where) and, even better, when is God going to choose our plan? Regardless of the expertise we have in planning, it does not compare to the perfect plan Jesus has to offer. Martha never dreamed she would get to see Lazarus come back to life right then. What a wonderful forerunner to Jesus' own resurrection, and Mary and Martha got to be there—up close and personal!

Go back to verse 14; Jesus says to His disciples, "Lazarus is dead, and for your sake I am glad I was not there, so that you may believe." In the time of Jesus, a person was not assumed really dead until three days had passed. Lazarus had been dead for four days, long enough that there was no explanation for his resurrection other than the miracle of Jesus. Jesus could have gone right away, and it would have been good. The people would have thanked Jesus; some would have believed and some not. But He waited for the right time, and what would have been good was now *great*. The power of God was the only explanation, and everyone believed.

On occasion, active compassion requires that we work with God in His perfect timing. God will always be looking for the way in which He will receive the most glory. In the midst of helping a friend or family member, we may want God to act *now*, but God may choose to act later for the greater glory.

A few years ago, I traveled from the missions field to the US with a missionary family who had experienced a loss on the field. The wife/mother had died from an allergic reaction. She left behind a husband and two young children. My youngest son and I traveled home with the family to help with the children. It was an incredibly long trip with so much sadness. Our last layover was in Memphis, Tennessee. As we flew over the city, we were met with storms. The weather was so bad that the pilot could not land the plane; we circled over the city for more than an hour. Finally, the pilot announced that we would make one more circle, but if we could not land, he had no choice but to divert the flight to Nashville.

I started praying, and like Martha, complaining. *God, how could You let this happen? This family needs to be home with parents and friends. Lord, do You know how they feel? You control the weather, why don't You fix this?!*

Surely Jesus cared for this family exactly like He cared for Lazarus; they were His missionary servants, and He loved them. Remember when Jesus went to see the dead body of Lazarus? Verse 35 says that Jesus wept. He was brokenhearted that this family went through so much waiting to experience the greatness that was about to happen when Lazarus was raised from the dead. It only made sense that He would be brokenhearted for this missionary family as they were in so much pain. So, why were we still flying around Memphis in a storm?

The plane finally landed in Memphis, but it was too late for the last flight to Oklahoma. This is where I saw God working His perfect timing. The travel agency had made a mistake that was not found until our arrival in Memphis. The children only had standby tickets from Memphis to Oklahoma and the flight had been completely full. Had we landed on time, we still would have been staying overnight in Memphis but at personal expense. However, because the flight was late, the airlines put the entire family in a five-star hotel for the night at airline costs. Landing in Memphis on time would have saved us a lot of anxious moments in the air and that would have been good. But then we would have missed the "miracle" in His provision of a very nice hotel and the protection from all the anxious moments that would have come from standby tickets. And I learned that active compassion sometimes means trusting in God's timing!

Sometimes when we care for others, we may not know the need or the plan, but we can know without a doubt that Jesus knows every need, He loves each one of us, He weeps for us when we are in pain, and He will do more than we can imagine in meeting every need. If we care through active compassion, someone may get to see Jesus be *great*!

❤ Have you ever tried to rush God? How did that turn out?

❤ Waiting on God's timing always results in God being great! What biblical stories can you find in which someone was required to wait on God's timing? (When David had a chance to kill Saul but did not have the go ahead from God, etc.) What results did their waiting bring?

❤ What lessons can we learn from their waiting?

Recently, I received an email entitled, *Perception*. The email was the story of an experiment done by a local paper. Joshua Bell, a famous violinist, was hired to stand in the subway playing his violin and wearing shabby clothes. Only a few people stopped to listen. Later, the subway audience learned who had been playing there all day. His violin was worth 3.5 million. Tickets to hear him play average $100 a seat. In their busyness, they had missed a high-dollar concert. The purpose was to point out the things we miss when we are in a hurry.

Don't miss the $100 performances that present themselves every day. We are so busy, we can easily miss something that can never be repeated—a surprise from God might be missed.

Don't miss the random acts of kindness. Nancy treating me to pie and Dr Pepper on Allen's first day of school. Gail, Wayne, Sandy, and Lou driving eight hours to attend a family funeral because of us. Chellie knowing just what to say after a difficult family situation. Jan sending a gift that arrived on a very stressful day. Connie's prayer telegram arriving on the day our city was taken under siege. Each one of these men and women were God's way of taking care of the little things exactly as He does with the birds of the air and lilies of the field. Active compassion is about taking care of the little things, like God takes care of the little things. Little is much when in the hands of God!

Don't miss your opportunity to be a God sighting for someone in need. My friend Sherry told me about a time at a homeless shelter when an elderly man was offering thanks for the food. He said, "God, we are so blessed and just when I thought there could not be anything else, You sent people."

Don't miss life and relationships. The American culture is busier than ever. We multitask, we go from early morning to late night, we walk around with some form of a "to-do" list, and we focus on getting through the day. In the midst of it all, I wonder if we miss $100 performances, acts of kindness, and God-sightings.

From Genesis to Revelation, God shows us the importance of relationships—with Him and with others. Eve was created for Adam to have relationship; Jesus spent His days on earth with 12 men for relationship; and God calls us daily to relationship with Him.

It is through ***relationships*** that we hear $100 performances—when our friend gives us the perfect advice, words of encouragement, prays with us, holds us accountable, cries with us, and laughs with us. When the words are just at the right moment it is equal to a $100 performance.

Because of ***relationships***, we experience active compassion, both as the receiver and as the giver: when we sit with a sick friend, when we take dinner to a friend who is on overload, when we babysit, when we receive a surprise gift, or when we share a cup of coffee. Even a text message can save the day. Active compassion—it's amazing!

It is through *relationships* that we perceive God at work; answering a prayer, changing a life, when we see a cancer patient find strength through God's grace, or when we see a friend remain kind to someone who was not so kind. Jesus tells us others will know we are Christians by our love for one another. Relationship itself is a God-sighting.

Regardless of our schedules, *relationships* are essential. Try it. You just might enjoy $100 performances, active compassion, and God-sightings. Don't miss this...*relationships*!

♥ List family members and friends who have provided hundred-dollar performances, acts of kindness, or been a God-sighting in your life. Pray a special prayer of thanksgiving for each of them today.

ACTS OF COMPASSION

❤ Libraries often need books read and recorded for the blind. Ask your local library if there is a need for readers.

❤ The blind often need transportation to the store, mall, or doctor's office. Contact the local society for the blind and offer to serve as a driver one day a month.

❤ School books in braille and braille signage, and specialized lab supplies are just a few of the needs for schools that teach blind students. Get together with a group of friends for a yard sale, using the proceeds to purchase some of these materials.

❤ Children who are taken from methamphetamine homes cannot take anything with them, not even their favorite toy, blanket, or clothes, because all items in the home are contaminated with hazardous chemicals. Gather with friends to make blankets and toys that police officers can give to these children. As you make the items, pray over each one, asking God to supply every need of the child that will use the blanket or play with the toy.

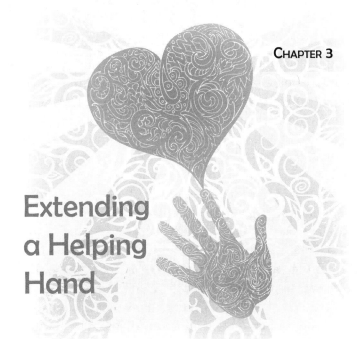

CHAPTER 3

Extending a Helping Hand

The paralytic had friends who cared enough about him to help. He was the poorest of the poor and the pity of many. But now, these men were going to take him to Jesus, the One he heard had the power to heal him forever! These four men were prepared to extend themselves to help their friend, to offer active compassion to this man who spent his days lying on a mat. They surrendered themselves to his need.

Jesus' telling of the story about the Good Samaritan in Luke 10:25–37 concludes that helping others *in His name*—the choice to surrender to active compassion—is His command to each one of us. Yet the Muslim is praying five times a day, giving alms to the poor, and trying to be a good person in order to earn eternal life. The Scientologist is trying to become a better person on personal merit. The Hindu is praying to multiple gods, hoping that one of them will be the provider of eternal life. And so, many people on the street simply hope that they have done enough good things to get to heaven. However, Christians know the only true answer: love Jesus.

"'Love the Lord your God with all your heart and with all your soul and with all your strength and with all your mind'; and, 'Love your neighbor as yourself'" (v. 27). Even though an expert in the Law knew the Law, he didn't recognize that he was standing before the very Son of God, the One he was to love with all his heart, soul, strength, and mind. He missed it! Because he missed it, his motive was not to learn the answer—Jesus—but to trap Jesus in a debate.

Does that sound familiar? How many debates have you found yourself in about religion and faith? There is nothing in Scripture that is outdated; it is still filled with true, relevant, and important directives for us on how to live a life that makes a difference today.

The law expert continued his questioning: "Who is my neighbor?" And, Jesus answered him with a story: A man traveling from Jerusalem to Jericho was beaten and left half dead on the side of the road. A priest and a Levite, both religious leaders, noticed the man on the road but chose to pass him by, leaving him beaten and bruised. Then a Samaritan passed by the beaten man and had pity on him. Like the paralytic's four friends, he put the rest of his day on hold and helped the man in need. He bandaged the man's wounds, took him to an inn, paid for his stay, and left instructions with the innkeeper for the care of the man. The Samaritan offered all this, expecting nothing in return.

When Jesus finished the story, He asked, "Which of these three do you think was a neighbor?" The expert knew the answer but choked on it: "The Samaritan." Jesus told him, "Go and do likewise."

A few years ago, I saw a young woman being beaten by a robber on the city streets of Baltimore. She was a nurse on her way home from work. She was on a scooter and had stopped for a red light when a young man ran up behind her, threw her off the scooter, and began beating her. He was trying to take her backpack and steal her scooter. Although I was a block away, I could see the entire incident. Other people were closer than I was, and I'm sure they could see what was happening, but I did not see anyone offering to help her.

Almost without thinking I swung my car around, drove closer to the sight, and ran to help her while dialing 911. The attacker ran off, leaving the young nurse beaten on the road. After the police took my statement, the officer commented, "She is fortunate that a friend was close by to help her." When I told him we had never met, he was shocked that I had left my car to help a stranger. Sound familiar? What a sad commentary on our culture today! We could learn a few things about helping others from the Samaritan.

So what all did the Samaritan do besides the obvious? *He was willing to help a stranger of another culture.* The Samaritan traveling from Jerusalem to Jericho was not in his home territory. This was not a friendly place for a Samaritan. He was in an area of cultural differences. The religious leaders of this time would not even speak the word *Samaritan,* because of disrespect.

Today, cultural differences are all around us and can be found in the most unexpected places. When we went to the Philippines, I knew there would be cultural differences. Filipinos point with their lips, raise their eyebrows to indicate yes, and are more concerned about relationships than schedules (a good difference, I might add). But sometimes the cultural differences in our own backyards are the ones that prevent us from being a friend. Cultural differences are frightening. But they are never an excuse for not sharing Jesus.

Think with me about cultural differences in any given city:

1. Body art versus no body art
2. Streaked hair color versus natural hair color
3. Nursing home smells versus fresh outdoor smells
4. Student verbal expressions versus traditional verbal expressions
5. Toddlers versus adults
6. Middle schoolers versus adults
7. Hispanics versus non-Hispanics
8. Southerners versus northerners
9. Vegetarians versus meat lovers
10. CEOs versus secretaries
11. Gang members versus non-gang members
12. Social drinkers versus nondrinkers

Hundreds, if not thousands of cultural differences could be listed. Make your own list. You might be surprised how long the list becomes. At the end of the day, there is only one cultural difference that matters:

believers versus nonbelievers. That is the one we are to be preeminently concerned about.

There are 6 billion people who do not know Christ. According to George Barna, 6 in 10 Americans do not know Christ. Islam is the fastest growing religion in America. I have to wonder if we, the believers, take eternal separation from God seriously. If we do, then this is one cultural barrier we will cross regardless of our fears.

For the adult believer, the adage "never talk to strangers" cannot be a way of life. My youngest son taught me a bit about this on a plane trip to Manila. We were on our way to Manila for him to have minor surgery. In front of us on the plane was a man from Australia. Jesse started the conversation with the man, asking if he would like to borrow his book, *The Cat in the Hat* by Dr. Seuss. Not surprisingly, the Australian said, "No thanks." But Jesse was persistent and kept up the conversation.

By the time we disembarked the plane, Jesse and the Australian man were good friends. When the stranger learned of Jesse's surgery, he asked for our address. By the time we returned home from our hospital stay, Jesse had a package from Australia waiting for him!

I'm not sure there was eternal significance in that brief friendship, but I know I decided to follow Jesse's example whenever I fly. Recently on a trip from Birmingham to Baltimore, I sat beside two men, one from South Africa and one from the Middle East. Somewhere in our casual conversation I was asked:

"You seem like a religious person. Have religious leaders in your faith made mistakes, and how do respond to that? You see, I am a Muslim but I am not happy with our leaders right now. Do you have any advice?"

Wow! The next two hours were spent talking about God's grace and how we can be holy enough to stand before God only when we are covered by the blood of Jesus. At the luggage terminal, the man asked, "Is there a church I might attend close to my home? What you have said makes more sense to me than anything I have been taught."

Jesse's conversation at four years of age might have been casual, but his example was my reminder to take advantage of every opportunity, even on an airplane. Following his example led to at least one conversation that I know ended with eternal significance.

❤ What cultures are you afraid of?

❤ What would it take for you to find the courage to cross those cultural barriers, whether the people are as close as next door or as far away as around the world?

❤ What strangers do you find yourself with periodically? Could you use that time to share with them a little about God's grace?

AN UNFAMILIAR PLACE

The Samaritan was not on his home turf. He was in a community unfamiliar to him. In today's world, we don't have to travel long distances to be in unfamiliar territory or to find someone in need. Sometimes an unfamiliar place is right next door. A new restaurant in your community may offer a different culture as well as unfamiliar food. A teen crisis center or a homeless shelter is unfamiliar territory for many of us. Christians find many unfamiliar places while on international missions trips. And a stateside missions trip can present even more unfamiliar territory.

An unfamiliar place can sometimes be an adjustment in our attitude. Deciding we will choose to let someone else take charge, let someone else be "right," let someone else have the remote (oh my!), be a little kinder to the cashier when the line is way too long. Extending a helping hand may feel unfamiliar and maybe even uncomfortable, but it speaks volumes.

John 13:35 says, "By this all [people] will know that you are my disciples, if you love one another." Do the nonchurch members at your church know you are the disciples of Jesus Christ by your love for one another? It is sometimes hard to love those we worship with. That may be the attitude that is the place of unfamiliarity.

Peter is a great example of stepping into unfamiliar waters, literally! Matthew 14:22–32 tells Peter's story of stepping out. The disciples were in a boat going to the other side of the Sea of Galilee when they spotted Jesus walking to them on the water. At first they were frightened, thinking they were seeing a ghost. Jesus told them who He was and to not be afraid. Peter, not so sure, called back, "Lord, if it's you, tell me to come to you on the water" (v. 28). Ya gotta love Peter! Jesus says, "Come." Peter got out of the boat. When he saw the waves around him, he was afraid and started to sink. He called to Jesus to save him. Jesus reached out and grabbed the hand of His friend and said, "You of little faith, why did you doubt?" (v. 31).

Jesus did not say to Peter that it would be easy to walk on the water. There were waves and wind. He simply told Peter to come. Nor does Jesus say to us today that all the places we go will be easy. There will be winds that toss us around. There will be waves that get us off balance. There will be boats that block our way. But the command is the same: "Come." And the promise is still true: "And surely I am with you always, to the very end of the age" (Matthew 28:20). "You of little faith, why did you doubt?" (v. 31).

❤ Read the story of Ruth and Naomi in Ruth 1–4. Where was Ruth willing to go that was unfamiliar?

❤ Why did she go?

❤ What impact did her decision have on Naomi?

❤ How did God guide her decision to go to the place that was unfamiliar?

❤ Make a list of the places or attitudes that you need to go to that are unfamiliar. Pray over each one and decide today to go there relying on Jesus' promise: "And surely I am with you."

GOING BEYOND CLEANLINESS

The Samaritan's task was not a clean undertaking. Remember, he dressed the injured man's wounds, which means he was willing to get another's blood on his hands and clothes.

Helping others is messy! Our hands get bloody, either literally or figuratively. Sometimes help is welcomed, but other times it is misunderstood. It can disrupt our day, affect our finances, take time away from family, or even expose us to hurt feelings. But it can also lead to someone's healing, someone's salvation, someone's self-esteem, or even someone's life.

Carrie McDonnall in her book, *Facing Terror*, talks about the strangers who were willing to get messy for her and how she was moved by their act of kindness. Carrie and her husband, David, were International Mission Board missionaries serving in Iraq. Following a survey trip, their car was caught in an ambush. David and three other missionaries in the car were killed. And, although Carrie was shot 23 times, she was alive. Once she was removed from the car, a man noticed her ankles were uncovered, a very immodest state by Muslim standards. He reached down and pulled her skirt over her ankles. That seems simple to us, but for this man it meant he was now unclean for prayers, because he had touched an unclean woman who was covered in blood. Would you, believer, be willing to do the same so that someone might have the chance to be covered in the blood of Jesus?

GO AND DO LIKEWISE

At the end of the passage, Jesus tells the expert, "Go and do likewise." We have the chance to go and do likewise every day in multiple ways. Active compassion is lived out when we pray, give, and go.

We go and do likewise when we pray. Sometimes the proof is in hearing the testimony of others. Recently, I had the privilege of hearing about answered prayers from a few of our missionary personnel.

A missionary serving in a difficult area stepped off a city bus, only to realize someone was following her. She was on her way to attend an underground worship service but decided to delay her travel until her pursuer was gone. In her effort to delay her travel ,she stopped and sat on a park bench. A stranger sat beside her and asked, "Are you an American?"

"Yes," answered the missionary.

"Then perhaps you can help me. Someone gave me a Bible a long time ago, and I am looking for help to understand the words. Can you help me?"

The prayer request the missionary had sent earlier was this: "Pray that God will help me find people of peace." God answered this by placing a young woman on a park bench. God was glorified when that young woman found salvation in Jesus Christ along with the rest of her family.

In another country, a missionary was hosting a medical clinic. An 84-year-old woman, bent over with pain for more than seven years, came to the clinic for help. She met a young worker who inquired about her relationship with God. She said God was someone she had heard about, but He would have to heal her for her to believe.

The young doctor shared Matthew 9 with the elderly woman and asked, "What would be easier? For God to forgive sins or to heal?" Without hesitation she responded, "To heal." The doctor prayed God would reveal Himself to her in a way that she would understand and recognize.

The next day, the woman returned pain-free and ready to receive Christ. Just like the healed leper, she shared what Christ had done with the 500 people waiting to see a doctor that day.

The missionary had sent a prayer request saying, "Pray that the medical clinic will bring glory to the name of Jesus." God answered the prayers by bringing healing. God was glorified by the testimony of an 84-year-old woman.

We go and do likewise when we give. Because people gave money to missions, my husband and I were able to help a newborn baby who had been infected with tetanus. By the time we learned of her condition, lockjaw had set in. The hospital in the Philippines required payment before treatment could be given. The family did not have the funds, so they came to us asking for help. We were able to use a portion of our salary to pay the hospital. Today this newborn baby has grown into a fine young woman who worships the Lord. Because someone gave, she is alive.

We go and do likewise when we go. A missionary was once asked by a volunteer if it would be better for the volunteer to send the money that he would spend in coming and stay in the US. The missionary replied, "No, when you come, you bring the presence of the Holy Spirit with you. There is no dollar amount on that!" We may not all go overseas but we can all go next door—to the coffee shop, to the lunchroom, or across the street. When we go, the presence of the Holy Spirit goes with us, revealing Jesus in us.

We go and do likewise when the change in our hearts makes an impact in the hearts of others. KP is a Filipino who was involved in a vigilante group whose purpose was to kill Muslims. He was angry and expressed that anger through violence. KP married a Christian who prayed for him daily and encouraged him to attend church with her. One night, he agreed to attend a revival service. KP met the Lord there. He surrendered his M16 and burned all of his spiritistic paraphernalia. He is now one of the leading evangelists in the country reaching out to Muslims, those who were once his enemies. Because of his changed heart, many other people have been changed.

💜 How are you "going and doing likewise"?

💜 Are you praying?

💜 Are you going?

💜 Are you giving?

💜 Is your life having an impact on the lives of others?

💜 Take a few minutes to read again the story of the Good Samaritan. What is the Holy Spirit leading you to do as a result of this parable?

"Isn't this the carpenter's son?" (Matthew 13:55). Can't you just hear this conversation? "Why, I knew him when . . . " "He was that little boy that ran around the street without his sandals." "Surely this is not the same boy!" "He could not be as wise as this!" The people could not imagine that the Jesus they knew as a little boy could be the same person as the man standing before them, showing such wisdom and power. Most likely they were thinking, "Who knew?" Who knew of His healing power? Who knew that He was the Messiah? Who knew that He was God's Son? Who knew that He had all that wisdom? All of us are guilty of being surprised when someone we've grown up with becomes someone extraordinary. The people of Jesus' hometown were no different.

Most of the time, those thoughts have few repercussions. But on this occasion, the consequences are huge! The passage even says, "They took offense at Jesus." And because they could not find the faith to believe that Jesus was who He said He was, He did not do many miracles in that place. How sad for those who needed His healing touch or His saving power!

Little Rock, Arkansas, is my hometown. And I have to wonder if my friends and family have ever said about me, "Who knew?" Who knew that my Savior is Jesus Christ, the very Son of God? Who knew that sharing the love of Christ with others is a top priority in my life? Who knew that my heart's desire is to know Jesus more and more every day?

Who knew that in my day-to-day life I pray that my character resembles that of my Creator? Who knew that I live in Baltimore, Maryland, because that is where my Lord has called me to serve? But most importantly, who knows Jesus because I was there?

What about you and your hometown? What about your church and its hometown? What do people say there? Who knows Jesus because you and/or your church are there?

For such a short passage in Matthew, it sure brings a lot of questions, concerns, and convictions. Do we overlook Jesus' work in our home state because of the believers' lack of faith? Are the churches in our home state small because of the believers' lack of faith? Are few people baptized in our home state because of the believers' lack of faith? Are missions efforts hindered because of the believers' lack of faith in giving, going, and praying?

It is my prayer that no work anywhere in the world will be hindered because of the believers' lack of faith. I want to have much faith so that Jesus can do many miracles here.

💜 Where is your hometown? Do the people there know about your relationship with Jesus?

💜 What is the reputation of your church where you live now?

💜 Are you living a life of faith so that Jesus can do many miracles where you are?

ACTS OF COMPASSION

The Good Samaritan was willing to go to someone of another culture who needed help. Regardless of where we live, there are people of other cultures living around us rather it be from another nation or another generation. Here are some ideas of how we can reach beyond cultures and help.

❤ Contact the state convention office in your state and ask about ESL (English as a second language) ministries in your state. ESL classes can be offered in evenings, on Saturdays, or Sunday afternoon. Consider using idioms as an opportunity to teach Bible. A great example: "The patience of Job" is a great way to tell the story of Job and the God he trusted.

❤ Volunteer at a local school (elementary, middle school, high school, or college) to help international students with homework, English, or learning their way around the area.

❤ Invite an international person living in your community to join you and your family as you celebrate Christmas. Consider decorating a Jesse Tree for Christmas as a way to reach lost and/or internationals. The Jesse Tree is a great way to tell the story of creation, Christ, and redemption. For information about the Jesse Tree go to www.beliefnet.com

or google "Jesse Tree" for sites with information on the history of, daily devotions, ornament ideas, etc.

♥ Volunteer at your local government offices in an effort to help guide internationals through the steps of becoming a legal citizen.

CHAPTER 4

Sharing Christ

The four men who carried the paralytic were willing to share Jesus with their friend. The conversation may have gone something like this:

Men: "Friend, we heard Jesus is in town."

Paralytic: "Tell me about this Jesus."

Men: "He is the promised Messiah. He has been doing miracles everywhere. Perhaps He can do a miracle for you."

Paralytic: "But I cannot walk. How can I get there? Are you sure He can help?"

Men: "We are sure! No need for you to worry, we will take you to Him."

Why is it so hard to share Jesus outside the church setting nowadays? In small groups, we talk about Jesus with no fear. Before and after church, we talk about Jesus. In committees, we talk about Jesus. But when it comes to talking to the cashier, a co-worker, or an acquaintance, it becomes much more challenging. Yet many of them need us to be willing to "take them to Jesus." Why are we hesitant to take them there? For me, it is more often than not a "growing" problem.

Growing plants is something I have never been able to do. If my friends want a plant to die, they just give it to me. Even while living in the Philippines, a beautiful tropical country, I could not grow anything. The only things that managed to stay alive around me were the palm trees that were already full grown.

When we returned to the US, our new home was in desperate need of new shrubs. Knowing I would need an expert to help with this project, I went to a nursery rather than a department store. I explained my problem in great detail. I wanted to be sure she knew I could not grow plants. She suggested that I purchase holly bushes, saying that they are very hardy and difficult to kill.

Difficult is not impossible; in just a few short weeks the bushes were dead. My oldest son was the first to notice the brown leaves. I was hoping they were just "adjusting" to their new home. No, they were dead.

If I could not keep holly bushes alive, I'm not sure what possessed me to buy ferns for our back porch. They were quick to die too. Determined to keep up with the neighbors who all had beautiful ferns, I purchased more ferns. Within a few weeks they were shedding and soon died. After the fourth round of purchasing ferns, I mentioned to a friend that I was quickly going through my savings account buying ferns. She had a great idea: "Purchase fake ones." They looked great and from a distance you could not tell they were fake. Well, that worked until an Arkansas tornado came along and blew them down the street. Now the entire neighborhood knew my ferns were not living ferns; they were fake ferns.

Sometimes as believers, we are tempted to hang the "fake ferns" of our spiritual life, rather than conquer those things that keep us from being alive and vibrant in our faith. Most of us know the right things to say, the right clothes to wear, and the right things to do. But somewhere along the way, we find ourselves looking "alive" when in fact it is just our "fake" fern. It is then that the thought of "taking someone to Jesus" requires more energy than we can find.

You see, once we tell someone we are Christians, our behavior has to match up with that statement. And that takes a lot of thought and energy. Suddenly, it matters how we treat the cashier. It matters if we participate in a gossip session. It matters when we are impatient with our co-worker. It is easier to hang our "fake fern" and not worry about it than to plant ourselves deeply in the soil of God's Word and the power it gives our lives. When I'm tempted to just hang out the "fake fern" for a while because I'm tired and weary, I remind myself of all the people around me who do not know Jesus. They do not need to see "fake ferns"; they need to see the real Jesus Christ living in me.

So how do we share Christ in the day-to-day and not be obnoxious? Not all of us are comfortable with asking things like, "If you should die today…do you know Christ?" And that is OK, because there are other ways to share Christ in the day-to-day activities of living life. One powerful tool is living out the fruit of the Spirit.

Galatians 5:22–23 says, "The fruit of the Spirit is love, joy, peace, patience, kindness, goodness, faithfulness, gentleness, and self-control." Notice, there is just one fruit but it encompasses many parts. We do not get to choose which ones we will keep and which ones we will leave out. They are all available through the Spirit! Believe me, there are days I would love to leave one or more of them out. But when all of them become noticeable in us, the Holy Spirit can use them to transform lives.

The following stories are real accounts about people who lived out the fruit of the Spirit when it was not so easy. They were living out active compassion through exemplifying love, joy, peace, patience, kindness, goodness, faithfulness, gentleness, and self-control. Each story represents a life changed.

LOVE
Annie Brown, a five-year-old who loved
unconditionally in the midst of brain cancer

"Jesus loves me! This I know, for the Bible tells me so" were written by Anna B. Warner in her book, *Say and Seal*. Not many today are aware of this book, but it was a best-seller. "Jesus Loves Me" is written as a poem being read by Mr. Linden, one of the characters, to Johnny Fax, a dying child, as a means of bringing comfort to the child. In its original form, the verses are:

Jesus loves me!
This I know,
For the Bible tells me so.
Little ones to Him belong;
They are weak, but He is
strong.

Jesus loves me!
This I know,
As He loved so long ago,
Taking children on His knee,
Saying, "Let them come
to Me."

Jesus loves me still today,
Walking with me on my way,
Wanting as a friend to give
Light and love to all who live.

Jesus loves me! He who died
Heaven's gate to open wide;
He will wash away my sin,
Let His little child come in.

Jesus loves me! He will stay
Close beside me all the
way;
Thou hast bled and died
for me,
I will henceforth live for
Thee.

Jesus loves me!
Loves me still,
Though I'm very weak
and ill,
That I might from sin be
free
Bled and died upon the
tree.

Chorus:
Yes, Jesus loves me!
Yes, Jesus loves me!
Yes, Jesus loves me!
The Bible tells me so.

Anna's father was a successful lawyer who lost everything in the Great Depression. The family left the
city and moved into a home they owned near West
Point Academy. Anna and her sister, Susan, began
writing for the income it provided. Along with her
writing, she also taught Bible studies at the academy
for the cadets. Her books, poems, classes, and hymns
were all an extension of her love, life, and legacy. Her
influence at the academy was so great that she is the
only non-military citizen buried in the West Point
Cemetery.

Ms. Warner's story is a tragedy that God turned into a victory. The financial crisis of the day brought her to the place where writing and teaching became a necessity. If writing had not become necessary, she may not have written the words to the song we have all sung and loved so much.

Throughout Scripture there are examples of God taking tragedies and turning them into victories in some of the greatest love stories ever told. The stories of Esther, Ruth, Lazarus, and Jesus are all reminders of God taking what appears at first glance to be horrific and taking it to a victory that none could have imagined.

Today, He still works through love in the midst of tragic situations. May 2, 2009, Annie Brown went to heaven to meet Jesus, whom she loved so much. Annie lived a very short life. She had just turned six years old when she went to meet Jesus. But that very short life had a very large impact on the lives of doctors, nurses, and hospital staff who met her. Annie's favorite song was Anna Warner's "Jesus Loves Me." She sang it every morning to the nurses and doctors who were treating her brain tumor.

In the midst of shots and treatments, Annie would say to the staff, "It's OK that it hurts. I love you." When she talked about her illness, she was not concerned about life or death because either way, for her, Jesus had won the battle. Jesus might choose to heal her, but if not, she would be in heaven making Him beaded necklaces and telling Him, "I love You, Jesus."

On May 7, almost 400 people gathered in Harrington, Delaware, to celebrate Annie's short life. Her physician's assistant said, "Annie fought a brave fight and showed lots of courage in her battle with cancer. But that will not be her legacy. Her legacy will be the unconditional love she gave us [the hospital staff] every day. Annie's voice saying, 'I love you!' will long be in our hearts. Annie, we will pass it forward."

Her service ended with the congregation singing "Jesus Loves Me." Who could have imagined that what was written as a poem in a book to comfort another dying child would be, years later, the testimony of a child with a brain tumor? "Jesus loves me; this I know." That was the reason for her unconditional love.

❤ Read the story of Esther and her love for her people. How did God use her to save an entire nation?

JOY
Monica Keathley, living joyfully as a paraplegic

In the fall of 2006, Monica was struck with a virus called *transverse myelitis*. She had a fever and was feeling weak. After a call to the doctor's office, it was decided that she should go to the emergency room for tests. Monica walked into the emergency room—feeling bad but walking. Thirty minutes later, she was paralyzed from the neck down, unable to breathe on her own. The next few months were uncertain for Monica, her family, and her friends. Every day was a challenge with Monica fighting for her very life.

In the midst of the crisis, Monica was determined that there would be a witness for Christ, regardless of her situation. Mouthing instructions to a friend, Monica had a sign placed on her door that read, "I serve an awesome God. Inquire inside." She still had the joy of the Lord in spite of her circumstances.

After a year in a rehabilitation center in Colorado, Monica returned to her home in Arkansas. Her church prepared her home to accommodate a wheelchair. Her sister and brother-in-law moved in, leaving their home in Missouri to become full-time caregivers.

Monica's friends bring her meals on occasion, take her shopping, read books, sing songs, tell stories ,and laugh. It is rare that Monica is not in church to worship on Sunday. In the midst of it all, her face is still full of the joy of the Lord. When I asked Monica about telling her story, she said this: "Just make sure that the readers know that I serve an awesome God who supplies all our needs. He has not forgotten even the smallest of my needs. God is good all the time."

Joy regardless of our circumstances is perhaps one of the strongest testimonies we can give. Monica's joy in ICU, in rehab, in the doctor's office, and at church speaks loudly as to who Christ is in her life to all who observe.

❤ Read Psalm 100 and reflect on all the reasons we have to be joyful.

PEACE
Gladys Parker, my mother-in-law

Gladys was an amazing mother-in-law! She did not miss a birth, an illness, a first of anything, or a big event at our church. Considering it was an eight-hour drive for her to get from Little Rock, Arkansas, to Oxford, Alabama, that is quite an accomplishment.

Later in her life, she was stricken with Alzheimer's disease, a devastating disease for the family as well as for the one suffering the ailment. We watched her go from a very together woman to a very weak woman who recognized nothing.

By the end, she no longer knew how to chew. We knew our time with her was short. My husband decided to read from his Bible a few of her favorite passages. He had only read a few lines when her eyes opened, and she began quoting what he was reading. She smiled and she was completely at peace. When she knew nothing else, she knew the Word of God.

Perhaps that is where peace comes from—knowing and trusting the Word of God. That is how Abraham was able to take Isaac up the mountain. It is how Jesus was able to go to the Cross. It is how we can be at peace, regardless.

❤ Read Paul singing in Acts 16:16–40. He was not worried about prison; instead of fretting, he was singing!

PATIENCE
Calvary Baptist Church, Oxford, Alabama

In the early 1980s, a prayer request came, asking churches to pray for an open door into the Soviet Union. The request was presented to the deacons at Calvary Baptist Church in Oxford, Alabama. At first there was skepticism, but the decision was made that the request would be a part of every worship service.

Year after year, Calvary, along with many other churches around the US, continued to pray, including our family, even after we left the US for the missions field.

Finally, in the fall of 1990, a door was opened; the Berlin Wall came down. In December 1991, the Soviet Union dissolved. Almost ten years of praying, but it happened. Patience means not giving up!

❤ Read the story of Job, perhaps the ultimate story of not giving up.

KINDNESS/GOODNESS
Thurman Braughton, retired missionary who served in Asia for almost 40 years

Thurman is one of the kindest men you will ever meet. It was his kindness and concern for others that compelled him to save a volunteer from another country, during a prison break. Thurman and the volunteer team had entered the prison for the purpose of conducting a Bible Study. The inmates had other plans, using this as an opportunity to escape from prison, taking hostages with them. One of the hostages was a young woman on the volunteer team. Thurman was able to get the gun away from the prisoner who was holding the young woman but, in the process, he was stabbed. Thurman recuperated from that wound in time. But the impact it had on the prison and on the young woman remains.

❤ Read Luke 21:1–4. How did this woman show her kindness and goodness?

FAITHFULNESS
Bill Hyde, retired missionary to the Philippines

Bill was often asked why he decided to stay in the Philippines for so long. This was usually followed by, "After all, you could die there." Bill's response was always: "Filipinos are worth dying for." Bill was faithful to his call to missions until the day he did, indeed, die for Filipinos. While he was standing at the Davao International Airport, waiting to pick up another missionary family, someone placed a backpack containing a bomb behind Bill. It exploded and killed Bill, but the size of his body saved many of those who were standing around him as he took the direct hit of the explosion. Just a few days after the bombing, a wreath was placed at the site where Bill had died. It read, "For the American who thought Filipinos were worth dying for."

❤ Read Daniel 6. How did he show his faithfulness? What were the results?

GENTLENESS
Dr. Jert Pingoy, missionary doctor with a vision

Although he had a thriving practice in Marbel, Philippines, he left it to treat the Muslims who lived just over the mountains. He literally took his office on the road. He purchased a van, which he turned into a makeshift hospital room. There he treated patients for almost every illness known to man and performed minor surgeries. As his gentle doctor hands treated hundreds of Muslims, his gentle spirit spoke with them about Christ the Messiah. It would be impossible to measure his success this side of heaven. Jert passed away a few years ago, but the influence of his gentle spirit still impacts the lives of those he served.

❤ Read Luke 1:43. Why do you think Elizabeth would be considered gentle?

SELF-CONTROL
Mr. Charo, dealing with a problem in a new way

Mr. Charo came to know the Lord while living in a very remote village in the southern Philippines. In the early days of his walk with Christ, he was faced with quite the challenge. Have you noticed how there seem to be major trials soon after we make a commitment to the Lord? It was certainly true for Mr. Charo. Mr. Charo was a farmer. He grew fruits and vegetables to support his wife and children. Around the property lines, he planted banana trees to provide income during the off-season.

A new family moved into the village. While the new neighbor was clearing his land for planting, he cut down the banana trees that were planted along the property line on Mr. Charo's side of the property.

My husband met Mr. Charo later that week while walking into his village. He and a few Filipino pastors were on their way to lead a seminar in Mr. Charo's church. Because Mr. Charo was one of the leaders in the church, they were surprised to see him walking away from the village. He explained that he would not be able to attend the seminar because he was going into the city to file papers against his neighbor.

He shared with the men about the loss of the trees and subsequent income. He feared he would not be able to provide food for his family without the income of the bananas. In that conversation, he also explained that, before he met Christ, his solution to the problem would have been much different. He would have killed this man for his actions. But because of his relationship with Christ, he knew that, regardless of his anger, he had to practice self-control and deal with the problem in a new way. His self-control literally saved a life from murder.

❤ Read about David's self-control in 1 Samuel 24.

REFLECTIONS

On occasion, my best friend, Jan, who lives in Monroe, Louisiana, mails me a "goody box" with all of my favorite things. Things like cold-brew coffee from New Orleans or a candle from a gift shop. This summer she added sandals to my gift box. It was great!

I wore the sandals over the Fourth of July weekend. At the mall, at the restaurant, at Inner Harbor, and in Canton, women stopped us and asked, "Where did you buy those sandals?" In Canton, two women were literally chasing us down to ask me about my sandals. Once they caught up to us they said, "Yes, we are stalking you because we want your shoes." Before the weekend was over, it became a family joke. "Who is stalking you now?"

As we walked home I had to wonder, "If people can stalk me down to ask about a cute pair of sandals, then why don't people chase me down because they see Jesus in my life?" What was it about the sandals that caused all the attention?

First of all, they are unique. They are hand-painted wooden sandals. The soles of the shoes are painted with hot-pink and lime-green flowers. The top of the shoes are lime-green with a hot-pink flower on top.

God made each of us unique. We all have different gifts and talents that are ours for the using. When David went to battle with Goliath, he did not rely on the armor of Saul to win the fight. He used his skills as a shepherd boy, because those were his talents given by God. Was it the expected talent for someone fighting a giant? Probably not. Most would have assumed that only a well-trained, mighty warrior could win this battle and that a shepherd boy with a slingshot would be killed instantly. But it wasn't David that God meant to get the glory; the glory was His. The Israelites had no question as to the power of God at the end of the battle. Only God could have used a slingshot to kill a very large, well-trained soldier!

When we stray from the uniqueness of who we are in Christ, we may miss an opportunity to experience a victory like none other. It is through our uniqueness that God gets to shine. David said in Psalm 139, "I praise you because I am fearfully and wonderfully made; your works are wonderful." If God's works are wonderful, and we are a part of His work, then we are, indeed, wonderful.

In today's culture, everyone is looking for that one thing that makes him or her unique and wonderful. Look no further—your very creation is unique and wonderful. When our thoughts, hearts, creativity, personality, appearance, demeanor, actions, and reactions are in line with who we are in Christ, then just maybe someone will chase us down to find out what makes us unique and wonderful.

Secondly—back to the shoes—they looked fun. In today's economic climate, life is stressful and hard. People are looking for relief from the stress. As believers, we have the solution—peace in Christ. Does that mean we will not be affected by the economy? No. One of my friends just lost her job. But the difference is that she knows God has been going before her, and

He will provide. She is at peace with the situation. In spite of the phone call from her boss this morning, she is still smiling this afternoon. My guess is, her co-workers, who received the same kind of call today, will be stalking her to learn how she keeps her smile and confidence in the midst of losing a job.

Each time I wear my sandals, I will wonder if I'm allowing my uniqueness to shine—so that God can shine. I will wonder if I'm showing peace and confidence regardless of my situation. I will wonder if I'm showing the world something that is worth stalking. My sandals will be too worn to wear one day, but Jesus is for all eternity. There is nothing more worth stalking than that!

❤ Read Galatians 5:22–23 again. Which fruit of the Spirit do you most frequently want to give back? What illustrations can you find in the Bible that encourage you to grow in those areas?

❤ Which fruit do you exhibit most? How do you use that fruit to minister?

❤ Who needs to see the fruit of the Spirit in your life?

❤ What are the things about you that are unique to just you? Do you allow that quality to shine so that God can shine?

❤ Living out the fruit of the Spirit is often a choice. It is choosing to have one attitude over another. It is about making conscious choices in the day-to-day routine that honor Christ through our attitude. While it is not easy, it can, and may be, the very thing that takes someone to Christ. That is active compassion at its best!

ACTS OF COMPASSION

Love: "What you have done for the least of these you have done for me" (Matthew 25:40). Keep ziplock bags in the car with peanut butter crackers, water, a gift card for fast food, a witnessing tract or prayer card, church bulletin, and so forth. Give them to the homeless in your community. Or provide stationery, devotional books, and similar items for the local jail.

Joy: Offer to host a birthday party each month for community service workers, such as fire and police personnel, teachers, and others. Take cupcakes and notes of gratitude for everyone.

Peace: People in crisis are looking for peace. Consider becoming a disaster relief volunteer. Information for service within the United States can be found at www.namb.net or internationally at www.baptistglobalresponse.com.

♥ Provide blankets and stuffed animals for children removed from drug-involved home environments or as a result of home fires. Contact the local police or fire department for information.

Patience: Volunteer at the local literacy office, and offer to listen to young readers in kindergarten and first grade.

Kindness/Gentleness: Call your local hospice agency to volunteer. Patients and their families need kindness and gentleness!

Self-control: Be an accountability partner for someone at a diet, rehab, or nutrition center. Consider offering a free exercise/nutrition class in your church. Promote with fliers. Use this as a chance to share Christ.

CHAPTER 5

Words in Action

The four men who helped the paralytic were not just speaking trivial words. They did not simply say they would take the paralytic to Christ—they did it! Their actions spoke louder than their words.

The adage "actions speak louder than words" is more true than most of us realize. According to researchers, our body language communicates 90 percent of what we are thinking and our words only 10 percent. So, if you really want to know how someone feels, learn to interpret body language!

This is the principle my dad knew well, even without higher education. He used to tell me, "Do as I say, not as I do!" He knew his actions were speaking louder than his words, and he wanted to be sure I had a clear understanding of which I was to follow.

There is another dimension to all of this that I think Jesus spoke to in His ministry. Christ wanted our actions and our words to give the same message. We see glimpses of that message in the Sermon on the Mount when Jesus says, "Simply let your 'Yes' be 'Yes,' and your 'No,' 'No'" (Matthew 5:37).

James, in his straightforward manor, says it like this, "Do not merely listen to the word, and so deceive yourselves. Do what it says" (James 1:22). We exemplify Christ when our knowledge, words, and actions all match! The four friends of the paralytic at that moment in time were communicating—through their knowledge (Jesus could heal), their words (we will take you to Him), and their actions (carrying the paralytic on his mat to Jesus)—the same message.

Most of us know that eating chocolate will cause weight gain, not weight loss. So why is it we still eat chocolate when we are on a diet? Our knowledge and actions are not lining up. Why? Because we want the chocolate! A dietician could get rich fast if she came up with a chocolate diet. Everyone would be willing to go on that diet.

Ministry is hard. We want our time. We want to do the things on our "to-do" list. We are tired and want a break. Basically, we want the "chocolate," and it is hard to give it up.

We want to lose weight with our whole heart but until we put into practice the rules of weight loss— limited sugar and regular exercise—desire alone will never be enough. Just like desire alone will not be enough to take care of God's "to-do" list. Recently, while speaking at a retreat, I met a young woman who had lost 110 pounds. By looking at her, you would have never known that she had ever had a weight problem.

I was in the chapel looking over notes for the next session when she walked in. All of the other women were eating French toast for breakfast. I commented that she was early and asked if she had eaten. She said yes and then told me about her weight-loss journey. She said French toast was her favorite breakfast, and she knew staying in the cafeteria would only lead to eating more than was healthy for her to eat. So, she left the temptation and came into the chapel early. Her knowledge, words, and actions were working together, and it was paying off in a big way. The weight loss made her feel better about how she looked, but more importantly, she was now healthier!

Our spiritual life is much the same. When what we know changes our actions and words, and our words and actions all work together, we are healthier spiritually and the world gets a wonderful picture of Jesus in our lives. Will it always be easy? No. We may still want the "French toast." Will we always do it without grumbling? No. I'm sure the young woman did not leave the dining hall—and French toast—without grumbling a bit. But, that is OK; the goal is to just do it. Jesus knows it is not easy, and He expects us to grumble on occasion. He even told a parable about it in Matthew 21:28–31. Take a minute to read the parable of the two sons.

When the father told the first son to work in the vineyard for the day, that son told his father that he would not do it. The son walked away, and then he realized his response was wrong. He went to the vineyard and worked all day. Notice, he did not go with a happy heart in the beginning. The parable does not tell us what his attitude was later in the day, but perhaps doing the right thing brought him joy and contentment.

The father told the second son to work in the vineyard for the day also. The second son responded with, "Sure, no problem." But he never showed up at the vineyard. His yes did not mean yes.

At the end of the parable, Jesus asked, "Who did the will of the father?" The crowd answered, "The first son." The first son did not start off so well, but eventually he did the will of his father. We might not get off to a great start, but that is not the important thing. What is most important is that we do the will of our Father, no matter how rocky the start.

Recently my youngest son, Jesse, was in a minor car accident in Philadelphia. His car had basically no damage, but the other car required some repair. The other driver put fault on Jesse. When the police and insurance agent talked to Jesse, they asked, "Were you in your lane?"

His response was, "I think I was."

"Can you say without a doubt you were in your lane?"

"I can say I'm 98 percent sure, but no, I can't say I'm 100 percent sure."

That being said, Jesse's insurance had to pay the claim from the other driver. Jesse was not happy with the decision. He felt he was being blamed for something that was not his fault. But Jesse was honest in his statement. He could have said he was 100 percent sure, and his insurance company would have fought the claim. But that would not have been 100 percent true, and for him to say something that was not 100 percent true would have been 100 percent wrong.

Jesse may not like the decision of the insurance company, but he can know that God is 100 percent pleased with his decision to be 100 percent honest. That alone is reason enough for Jesse to be 100 percent joyful.

Active compassion is not just what we do, but it is how we live. It is choosing to be honest when honesty is hard. It is choosing to carry the extra load at work with no pats on the back. It is choosing to honor God in every aspect of our life.

❤ Read James 1:19–27.

James encouraged us in this passage to be a reflection of Christ. By the standard of the world, what would be a "beautiful reflection" (financial success, good looks, etc.)? Now make a list of what we might see in the mirror of the "perfect law" (honesty, concern, etc.).

Check the words on the list in which you are 100 percent sure that your knowledge, actions, and words are in alignment. For the words without checks, claim victory through the power of Christ, and then check them off. It may require walking away from temptation (French toast), but the payoff will be worth it!

Now, read Matthew 21:28–31 again. Are there areas in your life that you have told the heavenly Father yes but not yet made it to the vineyard? Write an action plan of how you can and will do the will of the Father today.

KNOWING THE PROBLEM IS NOT ENOUGH

Knowledge is a good thing, but it is only a part of any process. The attorney general has stated emphatically that smoking causes cancer, yet people continue to smoke. Many of my family members are smokers. And that is just one of a thousand examples. One of my favorite examples comes from the Old Testament with Moses and Pharaoh.

Moses was instructed to give Pharaoh a message from the Lord. Pharaoh was to release the Israelites, or the water in the Nile would turn to blood. The Israelites were not released, and the water of the Nile was indeed turned to blood. This was Pharaoh's first encounter with the power of God. He was not totally convinced, especially when his magicians were able to make a match. And Pharaoh's heart began to harden towards the Word of God.

Moses continued to go to Pharaoh, asking for the release of the Israelites to prevent another disaster brought about by God—the next being an infestation of frogs. On the surface, that does not seem so bad. But just imagine not being able to take a single step without stepping on a frog.

I have never stepped on a frog, but two college friends of mine took me frog gigging, and I can tell you that a squished frog is disgusting. As a religion major at Ouachita Baptist University, many of my friends were young men preparing for the pastorate. We spent many long hours together studying Hebrew and learning to read from right to left instead of left to right. Two of those young men were David Uth and David Vandiver. One Friday night, we were tired of studying and very bored, so the two of them offered to take me frog gigging. I had never been before, and anything sounded better than studying.

What was I thinking?! We took a small flat-bottom boat to the nearby Ouachita River. I had the honor of sitting in the middle of the boat with the two Davids at either end. The frogs were croaking everywhere we turned. They knew we were in for a big "catch." I have always known that men are different in many ways than women, but I learned a big lesson that Friday night about men and hunting.

The two Davids would wait until a frog was getting ready to sound his song before stabbing them with the gig. It was at this precise moment that the frog would fill its body with air and the gig was likened to poking a hole in a tire. There was a loud shushing noise and the frog succumbed. I screamed, and they laughed. Many men and women are very different! There was nothing funny in my mind about this whole ordeal. It only took one frog for my frog-gigging experience to be complete. To this day, David Uth still gives me a hard time about frog gigging.

When I think of Pharaoh and the frogs, I think of frog gigging and that terrible noise made by the frogs. Everywhere the people walked and stepped on a frog, I'm sure there was that terrible noise. I think Pharaoh, even though he was a man, could not take it any more than I could. He called for Moses and asked him to pray to his God for the frogs to be removed.

God honored the prayer of Moses, and the frogs all died and were removed from the country. But as soon as God took the frogs away, Pharaoh went back to his old ways, and his heart became even more hardened.

Moses brought several more warnings from God with the result always being the same. The plague of gnats, flies, boils, hail, locusts, and darkness all came to Pharaoh. Moses continued to be faithful to bring the warning and to pray for God's help at Pharaoh's request. With every instance, Pharaoh was learning more and more about God. Pharaoh now had the knowledge that God kept His word. He even had the knowledge of the solution to all the problems: let the Israelites go. But his knowledge alone did nothing to solve his problems.

This story still happens today. People get in trouble, call on God, and then return to their old ways. Through the years, I have known people who have lived this way and suffered the consequences.

While serving in the Philippines, my husband spent many of his weeks hiking through the mountains with Filipino pastors, visiting villages that had never heard the message of Jesus. Those hikes were long and very difficult. Most of the mountains are very steep, and the weather is always hot and humid. The hikes would sometimes be as long as eight hours.

On one of those hikes, my husband was near the back of the line when, all of a sudden, the group stopped. He knew immediately that something was wrong. The pastor who was last in the line ran up to the front to find out what was wrong. The line had been intercepted by bandits who intended to do harm. The pastor told them of their purpose—trying to help others. The bandits not only decided to let them pass, they even traveled with them to the village to hear the message they had to share. One of the Filipino pastors had a long conversation with one of the men. The man responded, "If this message of Jesus is true, then it is something I want. But, Pastor, my family needs money. There is just one more place we are going to raid, and then I will quit and think about giving my life to this Jesus you have told us about."

The next day, the bandits left the village, and it was years later before my husband heard what happened during the bandits' last raid. The man who had said the next raid would be his last was killed in the raid. The military had been told of the bandits' plans and were waiting for them. The bandit had knowledge about Jesus, but that knowledge alone did not help him in the end.

This sad story is, unfortunately, the story of many people. But just as Moses was faithful to continue to give the message and continue to pray, we are to do the same. If we keep the knowledge to ourselves, it does not offer hope to anyone. God never intended for us to learn the Bible in depth and then never share its message in words, actions, and attitudes. The last words Jesus spoke before His ascension were: "you will be my witnesses" (Acts 1:8). A *witness* by definition is a person who offers evidence; a person who has personal knowledge of something; attesting to a fact or event.

Ask yourself these questions: Am I being a witness? Do I give evidence of Christ in my life? Do I have personal knowledge of Jesus? If you answer yes.

then you are a witness in Jerusalem, Judea, Samaria, and the ends of the earth.

After Jesus was taken into heaven, the men stood there, staring into the sky. If I had been there, I would have been doing the same. But then, two men dressed in white [apparently angels] came. "'Men of Galilee,' they said, 'why do you stand here looking into the sky?'" (Acts 1:11). On occasion, I wonder if the church is standing looking into the sky when the instruction was "be my witnesses."

❤ Read Exodus 7–10.

❤ Write each plague that God brought to Pharaoh. Beside each plague, write Pharaoh's reaction, Moses' response, and the reason Pharaoh's heart became more hardened each time.

❤ Are there areas in your heart that are hardened? Do you find it difficult to love an AIDS patient? A gang member? A militant Muslim? A prostitute? A teenager in trouble? A fellow church member?

❤ Pharaoh was not one of Moses' favorite people, yet Moses continued to be faithful and pray in the midst of that difficult relationship. Add to your prayer list the people or people groups you have trouble relating to or loving. You might be surprised at the result.

KNOWING THE SOLUTION IS NOT ENOUGH

Pharaoh and the bandit both knew the solution to their problems. But because they did not act on what they knew, the knowledge was not helpful. For Pharaoh, it meant coming to the last plague he would face—the plague of the firstborn.

Exodus 11 tells about the plague that took the life of Pharaoh's son. He was devastated, and in his despair, he released the Israelites. He even asked for Moses to ask God to bless him. At this point, Moses began the journey of leading the complaining Israelites out of Egypt and into the Promised Land. There were approximately 600,000 men, plus women, children, and livestock. What a journey it must have been!

First of all, God did not take them by the shortest route. If they had taken the shortest distance, they might have found themselves in battle with the Philistines, probably causing them to choose returning to Egypt instead of moving forward. So, God took them through the desert toward the Red Sea. The shortest way is not always God's way.

While the Israelites were traveling, Pharaoh had a change of heart and decided to send his army after the Israelites. The Israelites found themselves between a "rock and a hard place" in the form of the Red Sea and the Egyptian army. What did they do? Complain to Moses, of course. They asked, "Did you bring us here to die?" If I had been Moses, I might have thought death to be better than listening to more than a million people complain!

As a new missionary, I remember thinking on occasion that God had simply brought me to the Philippines to die. Not because of the danger that was around on occasion, but because sometimes it was hard. Within our first six months, our oldest son and I had *dingy fever*; our youngest son had *hookworm*; there was a coup in our city; we had two earthquakes measuring over 7 on the Richter scale; and my husband had *amoebic dysentery*. All that, and we hadn't been there a year! Like the Israelites, I asked God, "Did you bring us here to die?!"

Obviously, we did not die. But I did learn first-hand about the power of God. None of us had side effects from our illnesses. Not a single plate was broken in either earthquake. During the coup, another family stayed with us, and we ate fudge, popcorn, and watched movies for three days—a wonderful break from language study. As a matter of fact, we had a great time over those few days. We developed a relationship with a Filipino family that would have never grown to the best-friend level without the coup.

Most importantly, our neighbors saw God work in miraculous ways. They were introduced to the power of God by watching us live through those very things that I found myself complaining to God about. They saw how God blessed us by providing for every need—health, safety, and friends.

When life gets hard, we are all tempted to complain and look for blame. God reminds us that in our weakness, He will make us strong. The Israelites only had the promise of delivery at this point in time, but God was there to complete the promise. Their role was to be faithful and let God take care of the rest.

God brought a cloud to block the view of the Egyptian army, and through the rod of Moses, He parted the Red Sea for the Israelites' safe passage. Moses knew the solution, and he applied it to the problem. As a result they were saved.

Pharaoh, on the other hand, had just the opposite experience. He lost his entire army. He could have prevented that from happening if he had only followed through with what he knew to be the solution to his problem—let the Israelites go.

The four men who carried the paralytic to Jesus applied the solution to the problem. The problem was a paralyzed friend. The solution was Jesus. They made an action plan to get the problem to the solution.

As Christians, we know the solution to any problem is Jesus. Our role is to follow through with an action plan that gets the problem to the solution. For each of us, those problems will be different, both in our own lives and in the lives of those we touch each day. But for all of us, the solution has been, is, and will be Jesus Christ.

What if the four men had walked by the paralytic that day and said, "Jesus could heal you," then kept walking? What if Moses had not used his rod to part the Red Sea? The ending to the stories would have been vastly different. If my friend Carolyn had not introduced me to Jesus, I wonder what my story would be today. I wonder if my ending would be different.

I met Carolyn when my family moved to Little Rock, Arkansas. It was the last six weeks of my ninth-grade year. I was not happy about the move. This would be my twelfth school in nine years. I wanted to stay in Nashville, but God took me a different route to bring me to Him. Carolyn sat in front of me in home-room and, every day, she invited me to attend church with her. Every day I turned down the offer. My heart was hard. One day, she said the magic words for a 15-year-old, "We have the cutest guys in our youth group." Just like Jesus met the woman at the well where she was, Carolyn met me where I was. The fol-lowing Sunday, I went with Carolyn to church.

There were cute boys there, but what I noticed most was the presence of God. John 13:35 says, "By this everyone will know that you are my disciples, if you love one another." I didn't know why the people there were so different, but I knew whatever it was they had, I wanted. I returned every Sunday, hoping it would rub off on me. Eventually, I learned what they had was a relationship with Jesus. As soon as I learned what it was, I took action to get it. I took a deep breath, stepped out into the aisle, and made my way to the pastor. My life story changed for eter-nity that day. I'm thankful that Carolyn acted out her active compassion and shared the message of Jesus with me. I learned God's truth through Carolyn: *God so loved me that He gave His only Son Jesus, so that if I believe in Him, I will not perish but will have eternal life.* Who can you teach that to today?

❤ Take a few minutes to write your testimony. Who introduced you to Jesus? Where were you when you asked Him to be Lord? Say a prayer of thanksgiving for that person who first shared Jesus with you.

❤ Make a list of those times in your life that you know God was demonstrating His power through your circumstance. Someone you know may need to hear that story. Write their name and pray for an opportunity to share your experience of God's power with them.

❤ Missionaries live out their lives every day in view of others. Pray that God will use their daily experiences to show Christ's power in their lives.

REFLECTIONS

Moses used his rod to accomplish many great things for God. It became the tool for God to use in speaking to problems and solutions. But before Moses could use his rod for God's work, he had to lay it down.

My husband has a pair of jeans that are faded, torn, and too tight. Every spring when I clean out closets, I ask if we can throw away those jeans. His reply is always, "No, don't throw those out; they are still good." Good is a matter of perspective.

Most of us have things that we hold on to—a favorite item or something that has sentimental value or reminds us of something in the past that we don't want to forget. There is nothing wrong with that. But every once in a while, there are things in our lives that we are called on to lay down.

Take a moment to read about Moses' rod in Exodus 4.

> Moses answered, "What if they do not believe me or listen to me and say, 'The LORD did not appear to you'?"
>
> Then the LORD said to him, "What is that in your hand?"
>
> "A staff," he replied.
>
> The LORD said, "Throw it on the ground."
> —Exodus 4:1–3

The rod turned into a snake until Moses picked it up by the tail, and then it turned back into a rod. At the end of that encounter, God said to Moses, "This . . . is so that they may believe that the LORD . . . has appeared to you" (Exodus 4:5).

From that moment forward, the rod possessed new strength. Moses used it to part the Red Sea and lead the Israelites out of captivity. The rod had been Moses' tool, but it became God's tool.

Brian Pruitt, a former football player for Central Michigan University, tells about letting go of football for a while. Brian was a sought-after player in high school but was disqualified his freshmen year of college because of low grades. He had to lay down his football. When he picked it back up, it wasn't his anymore; it was God's. God took that year off to prepare Brian for the fame and publicity he was about to receive. Brian was no longer a football player but a Christian who played football.

In my own life, there have been a few times when God said to me, "What is that in your hands? Lay it down." Each time was hard and came with struggles, causing me to question. But in the end, there was new strength.

There was the time when we were leaving the missions field to come home permanently. There were Filipinos in my hand, and I didn't want to lay them down. They were lost and needed to hear the message of hope. It was hard to let go, but it was also clear that God was calling us home and asking me to let go of what I was so desperately holding on to. Once I let go, God did amazing things. We left 23 churches, and now there are almost 50. I still have the privilege of telling the God stories more than ever before! And I live next door to a Filipino, the very people group I laid down. God is full of surprises! The stories in the Philippines are no longer about the missionary who had lived there, but about God who stayed there.

What is that in your hand? What is the talent, gift, resource, job, or person that you are holding in your hand? Do you have a tool that needs to be God's tool? Is God asking you to lay it down? No worries—when He tells you to pick it up again, it will have new strength that can only come from God, and they will "believe that the LORD…has appeared to you."

ACTS OF COMPASSION

💜 What is the talent, gift, or resource that you hold in your hand? Consider laying it at the feet of Jesus today.

Walkers/Runners: Sponsor a walking/running club at your church. Before the members head out, give them a list of prayer requests from missionaries and ask them to pray as they exercise. Use this as an opportunity to prayerwalk the neighborhood around the church. Pray for each house the team passes by. Provide weekly memory verses. It is amazing how fast a walk/run goes by when our minds and hearts are busy!

Musicians: Offer free classes in underprivileged communities or in schools without the funding for music programs.

Accountants: Offer budgeting or finance management classes for a Christian Women's Job Corps and a Christian Men's Job Corps (information can be found at www.wmu.com), in a low-income housing area, or at a local business.

Crafters: Provide free holiday craft seminars for the community. Many craft stores will donate supplies if asked.

Knitters/Crocheters: Make hats and blankets to comfort cancer patients. Body temperatures may lower during chemotherapy. Attach a Scripture verse and prayer for much-needed spiritual comfort!

Mechanics: Provide oil-changes and car check-ups in low-income communities or for single moms who need help.

Beauticians: Provide free haircuts for lower-income families in the area.

Carpenters: Provide a day of handyman skills for the elderly in the community.

Gardeners: Unused produce can be given to local charities that provide meals for the homeless.

God can use every skill and willing hand. We only have to be willing to let go!

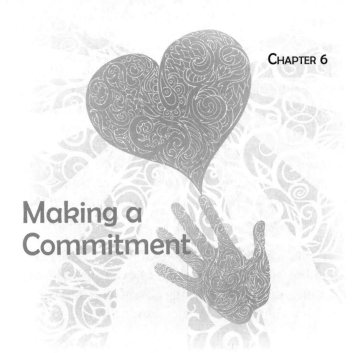

CHAPTER 6

Making a Commitment

The four men who helped the paralytic were committed to taking their friend to Jesus. Once they started on the journey, they were determined to go all the way. The paralytic was on his way to being healed ,because they were committed to getting him there.

We all deal with commitment every day. Marriage. Raising children. Careers. Ministry. All of these require a deep level of commitment. Imagine if a betrothed were to say at the altar, "I do—for now— but I might change my mind later." None of us want to enter a marriage, or even an engagement, without commitment. Pastor and author Rick Warren says that shortly after his wedding, he told his wife that he didn't *feel* married. His wife assured him: while he might not *feel* married, he better *act* married. That is part of commitment, no matter what it feels like. We *act* on the commitment, not the *feeling*.

Because our three boys grew up on the missions field, they had many unusual pets. Allen, our oldest, was the real caregiver when it came to animals. When a small lizard got stuck on mouse paper, Allen was the one who wanted to get it off the paper and back into the grass. Just let me say, a little dishwashing detergent goes a long way. That lizard was the cleanest lizard in all the Philippines by the time we had it set free from the mouse paper!

Along with lizards, there were pet chickens, birds, a monkey, and of course, dogs. One of our dogs had the same markings as a tiger, begetting his name. Tiger was Allen's dog. Wherever Allen was, Tiger was close by.

Dogs in the Philippines are part of the security system. Tiger lived outside. One night, someone decided to break into our car. To get past Tiger, they fed him MSG stuffed inside meat. MSG is not a good thing for dogs. It causes their blood pressure to rise rapidly and can lead to stroke or death. Tiger suffered a severe stroke.

Most likely, he should have been put down, but Allen would not even talk about it. Instead, he made a commitment to take care of Tiger every day. He fed him tiny bits of food by hand, and he used a dropper to give Tiger water. Every day that Allen cared for Tiger, his strength started to return.

Months later, Tiger was eating by himself, walking again, and playing with Allen again. It was as if he was determined to regain his strength for Allen. For the rest of Tiger's life, Allen was committed to taking care of him, and Tiger was committed to getting well for Allen. It was amazing to watch!

Tiger lived for a few more years. We did not expect him to make it a few more days after the stroke. I have no doubt that he lived those years because of Allen. It was a wonderful picture of commitment.

❤ What commitments do you need to make? Are you willing to go the distance?

NO COMPLAINTS

In all those weeks and months that Allen took care of Tiger, not once did he complain about the work it involved. He might on occasion complain about homework or household chores, but the day-to-day care for his dog was something entirely different. The lesson to learn here is, when you are in the midst of helping someone, *don't complain*. For the recipient of the care, that is a very unpleasant place to be. Our help will not be as meaningful.

Tiger was not Allen's first trial. Allen was born with a birth defect called Poland's syndrome. Poland's syndrome ranges in severity but, for Allen, it meant the lack of development of his left hand. When he stretched out for the first time, the first thing I saw was his left hand. Parents of newborns talk about counting fingers and toes, but there were no fingers to count on his left hand. He was rushed to an examining room where specialists could examine his heart and lungs. My doctor was working frantically to get his job done, so that I could have some answers. When he finished his part of the job, he took my hand to tell me about the problem we were facing.

I'm not sure who was crying more, me or my doctor. I also remember knowing, without a doubt, no matter how painful this was, that God would use this for His glory.

By Allen's first birthday, he had gone through 6 surgical procedures. By the time he was 5, he had been through 11. Although his birth defect is still noticeable, the surgeons were able to build Allen a hand with fingers. Most people think he has been badly burned. Through it all, I have learned so much from my oldest son and the grace of God.

Allen was three months old when he had his first surgery. As Allen was carried to surgery, I felt totally helpless. I could not save him from this. I could not go in his place. I could not help with the surgery. All I could do was to wait and pray. And what a wait it was! Allen was in surgery for seven very long hours. That was his shortest time in surgery. The others took as much as ten hours.

This tiny little baby with an IV in his foot and the biggest cast I have seen on his arm woke up smiling as if everything was normal. As the year went on, I watched him learn to crawl with his arm in a cast. He learned to walk with his arm in a cast (that was quite the balancing act). He said his first words with his arm in a cast. At the end of every trip to the hospital, he was still smiling, still playing, still enjoying life, and still stealing the hearts of his nurses with his sweet disposition and long eyelashes.

Gradually, because of the commitment of the surgeons, Allen was getting a hand. But something else was happening with every trip as well. God was working while we were waiting out those long hours of surgery. Children's Hospital in Birmingham,

Alabama, is full of parents who are searching for hope. They are there with children facing cancer, serious birth defects, and serious injuries. Many of the parents have no church affiliation at all. My husband and I had the opportunity to pray with those parents, cry with those parents, and share Christ with those parents. Our commitment was to honor God through our trial.

I know Allen has had some hard times, even though he never complained. He has had to endure questions, stares, thoughtless comments from young children, and the frustration of not always being able to grip with the strength needed. While I've watched, I've sometimes cried for my son.

I have also watched him overcome difficulties because of his commitment not to be hindered by his birth defect. He learned to play piano, only struggling when he had to reach an octave. He played basketball, baseball, and football. Now that he is grown, he still plays volleyball and paintball. He graduated college with a degree in biology and currently works in a lab handling delicate equipment every day. While I've watched, I've rejoiced in and marveled at God's grace.

And sometimes I've watched God bring us the strangest surprises. After arriving in the Philippines, we met an older missionary couple, the Millers. Their daughter was married to a surgeon in America, and the young couple came to visit her parents. Because our children were similar in age, and we lived close to the beach, the Millers brought their daughter and her family to General Santos to visit for a few days with our family. The surgeon's son-in-law "just happened" to be an orthopedic surgeon. When he looked at

Allen's hand, he recognized the work immediately. He had been one of the surgeons that had assisted in Allen's surgeries when he was a baby. Only God brings the perfect doctor halfway around the world for a much-needed check up! We were all happily surprised!

While he was growing up, Allen inspired me almost every day. How could I complain when he so enjoyed life? How could I complain when I never heard him complain? It was his life that helped me come to the place that I can be joyful in all circumstances.

"Rejoice always, pray continually, give thanks in all circumstances; for this is God's will for you in Christ Jesus" (1 Thessalonians 5:16). Allen has lived that verse out in the way he has dealt with having a birth defect. God has been glorified through his life, and I have been blessed to be his mom. One day, a woman will be blessed to be his wife, and a child will be blessed to have him as a dad. And one day, he will see how many people met Christ through his trial, and he will be blessed.

"Give thanks in all circumstances for this is God's will for you in Christ Jesus" (1 Thessalonians 5:18). This verse also had meaning for the four friends who helped the paralytic. The ministry God had called them to would be hard. They were going to get tired, dirty, and sweaty. In the midst of it all, they were to give thanks.

God may have called you to a task—to do something or help someone—that is hard. Not every task is pleasant. Not every job is neat. Not every assignment can be finished in a short time-span. Sometimes we hear complaints instead of thanks; we get dirty;

we get tired; and the hours are long. And still we give thanks because this is God's will.

💜 Spend some time today reading Psalms. Underline each time the psalmist uses the phrase *give thanks*.

💜 "Count your blessings, name them one by one" are the words found in a very old hymn. Counting our blessings is a good reminder of the grace of God. List your life's blessings. List them in two categories: blessings that have come through trials, and blessings that have just come (ex: children, house, etc.). On a bad day, look at your list and be blessed.

💜 Take time now to read Hosea 3.

💜 Even though Hosea's wife had been unfaithful in marriage, Hosea was still committed to her and their relationship. Similarly, God was committed to Israel in spite of all her shortcomings.

We can never control what someone else does, but we can control what we ourselves do. It is our responsibility to keep our promise of commitment. With whom and what have you committed your life?

💜 Are there commitments in your life that need renewal? Write them on sticky notes and attach them to the bathroom mirror as a reminder.

GIVING UP IS NOT AN OPTION

I have one primary rule for choosing a movie: there must be a happy ending. If the movie does not have a happy ending, then I just do not watch the ending. Life comes with enough sadness; there is no reason to experience that in a movie. If I am going to watch a movie, I want to escape to fantasyland where music is played with the first kiss, the right girl finds the right boy, no one is sick and no one is hurt, and everyone lives happily ever after.

One of my favorite movies, even though it is not a love story, is *Apollo 13*. It amazes me that the writers and actors keep the movie suspenseful, even though the audience knows the ending. Every time I watch it, I wait with anticipation for the safety of the astronauts.

In the movie, Ed Harris makes the statement, "Failure is not an option." It was that mind-set that took the scientists and engineers to a new level of thinking about and solving the problems they were facing.

The four men who helped the paralytic set out with that same mind-set: "failure is not an option." It is sometimes called determination, hard-headedness, or stubbornness. But, whatever it is called, it is sometimes what is required to get the job done.

In the New Testament, Peter is one of those people who was probably a bit hard-headed and stubborn. Sometimes this led him to failure, but sometimes it led him to victory. More often than not, it took several tries for Peter to get it right. Or maybe I should say, three seemed to be the magic number for Peter.

Three of his life lessons involved three tries. In Matthew 26:69–75, we read that Peter denied Christ three times. Three times Jesus asked, "Peter do you love me?" (John 21:15–17). In Acts 10:9–16, the sheet rose and fell three times in Peter's vision before he understood the message.

Perhaps Peter's most difficult lesson is described in Matthew. As he is listening to Jesus tell of His upcoming death at the last supper, Peter vows he will never deny Christ, no matter what the cost. His stubbornness was shining through! Jesus knew what was to come and predicted Peter's actions. A pastor interpreted these verses in a way that was new to me: could it have been that Jesus was giving Peter a warning? "Stay away, Peter, you cannot handle the temptation that is going to come to you." I'm not sure if Jesus was giving a warning, prediction, or both. But it is a lesson for all of us to heed. None of us intend to deny Jesus through our actions but, in the face of temptation, it can happen. Certainly it happened with Peter. Three times he denied his relationship with Jesus. When he realized what he had done, he wept.

Peter could have prevented that experience if he had either avoided the temptation or stayed true to his knowledge of Jesus. No doubt he learned a lesson that night that led to more of a life of victory.

In John 21, we read the conversation where Jesus asked Peter, "Do you love me?" Jesus was asking do you *agape* me? *Agape* is Greek for unconditional love. It loves regardless of relationship, action, benefit, and so forth. It is the kind of love Jesus has for those who call Him Lord. It is the love that took Jesus to the Cross. Peter responded with, "Of course I *philos* you." *Philos* is a friendship kind of love. Certainly that was an appropriate kind of love between men who were close friends. But Jesus was asking for more, He was asking for *agape* love. It took Peter a while to understand what Jesus was asking. He even got rather frustrated in the conversation. But eventually, Peter got to the place of knowing that his love for Jesus would have to be an *agape* kind of love if he was to find victory in his ministry.

Then, in Acts 10, we read about Peter's vision. A man named Cornelius had a vision of an angel telling him to send men to Joppa to bring Peter to Caesarea. Cornelius sent three men to find Peter. As the three were traveling, Peter had a vision of unclean animals that he was to kill and eat. Peter could not believe that God would ask him to do such a thing! After all, this would be in direct violation of Jewish law. Peter was missing what God was trying to tell him, twice!

Up to this time, Peter had only witnessed to Jews. After seeing the vision for the third time, Peter finally got the idea. He was asking him to look past his Jewish culture and take the message of Christ to every tribe. In God's perfect timing, the men of Caesarea showed up at Peter's gate. Peter accepted their offer to go to the house of Cornelius. After his arrival, Peter started his message to Cornelius and his household with the words in verse 34: "I now realize how true it is that God does not show favoritism but accepts from every nation the one who fears him and does what is right."

Prior to this event, Peter had preached his most famous sermon in which 3,000 came to know Christ (Acts 2). It took seeing a vision three times, but once he got, it he got it! His ministry exploded.

"Failure is not an option" is a great quote and a good mind-set when we have God's understanding of what failure is and is not. Some would see Peter's denial of Jesus as a failure. But I see it as anticipating victory, because of the lesson he learned. It was through this event that he found compassion. It was through this event that he learned to heed the warnings of Christ. It was through this experience that he learned about victory that is found in Christ alone. Anything that teaches us about the power we have through Christ results in victory, not failure.

Like Peter, all of us have lessons we *have* learned and lessons *to* learn. There are some points in our lives that we may see as total failure. Maybe a missed opportunity to share Christ. Maybe a bad choice. Maybe giving in to a bad attitude. But if we learned anything about God's grace, power, and victory, then the experience was not an absolute failure. It was instead an experience that led to victory.

❤ Read 1 Peter 4.

❤ What does Peter say in verse 19 about commitment?

❤ Read Hebrews 12.

❤ Winning the race requires focus, perseverance, and commitment. What advice does the author of Hebrews give to help us finish the race?

❤ What are the similarities between these verses?

❤ What steps will you take to be committed to finish the tasks He has for you?

REFLECTIONS

Do you enjoy watching the outtakess at the end of a movie? Actors say the wrong lines, use the wrong name, or sometimes trip over their own feet. Watching actors make multiple mistakes always brings lots of laughter. In real life, however, multiple takes to get something right is not so funny.

My family and I were returning to Butuan after finalizing visa papers in Manila. We boarded the 737 jet and fastened our seatbelts, preparing for departure.

Take One: The pilot started down the runway, increasing speed for take-off. Just when we should have been leaving the ground, the pilot put on the brakes. Every passenger on the flight was thrust forward, hitting their heads on the seats in front of them. Then the announcement came, "I'm sorry folks, we are not showing full engine power for take-off. Not to worry; we will try this again." I remember thinking, *I would rather you didn't!*

Take Two: The pilot taxied the plane down the runway and started for take-off. Once again, he applied the brakes just before the end of the runway. This time, the passengers were taken back to the terminal to wait while mechanics worked on the plane. Hours later, we could once again board the plane.

Take Three: The pilot taxied out, revved up the engines, and headed down the runway. We were all holding our breath in anticipation. This time, we easily left the ground. At the end of that trip, I decided one take is much nicer when flying!

Peter was a man who often required multiple takes. Three of his life lessons involved three takes. In Matthew 26:69–75, Peter denied Christ three times. Three times Jesus asked if Peter loved Him (John 21:15–17). In Acts 10:9–16, the sheet rose and fell three times in Peter's vision before he understood the message.

In these three different instances, Peter missed what Jesus was trying to tell him at least twice. To his credit, Peter was committed to getting it right, so he kept trying. Because of his commitment, Peter learned one of his most important lessons: Jesus was not just the Savior for the Jews, but He was the Savior for all people. That was the lesson which led to the miraculous results in Acts that took the gospel message all around the world.

Today there are people all around our globe who fear God and do what is right in their own culture. Koreans spend hours in prayer as they are taught dedication and a strong work ethic. Others around the globe show bravery in leaving their family's faith, knowing the cost could be their very lives. Africans turn their backs on superstitious teaching of witch doctors to follow the true teaching found in Scripture. Some Hispanic cultures start revival at 10:00 P.M. rather than our usual time of 7:00 P.M.

In America today, we are exposed to almost every culture. Do they all know the one true God? Probably not. We have more opportunities than ever before to reach past our American culture from our own backyard and take the message of Christ to many "tribes." I pray we will all be committed to reaching beyond our own cultures, whether that be Western,

Asian, or Hispanic, and enjoy the blessing of multiple cultures worshipping together. This is one take I would like to get right the first time. "For God so loved the world that he gave his one and only Son, that whoever believe in him shall not perish but have eternal life" (John 3:16).

ACTS OF COMPASSION

Most of us are willing to do random acts of kindness. Many are willing to leave the comfort of home for a few days on a mission trip. But when it comes to direct evangelism, we shudder with fear. Yet evangelism allows us to tell others the way to salvation. Without a willingness to share Christ, our acts of compassion fall short!

❤ Practice telling your salvation experience. Memorize it. Write it. Commit to telling your "God story" to at least one person this week. Ask a friend to be your accountability partner in this endeavor. Pray that God will lead you to the person who needs to hear and follow His leading.

❤ Memorize a few key Scriptures to employ in sharing the gospel. Romans 3:23, 6:23, 5:8, 10:9, 5:1, and John 3:16, 14:6 are well-used verses. Include in this list your life verse. All of us share most naturally from our own experiences.

❤ Use a piece of jewelry, clothing, or a wristband that lends itself to presenting the plan of salvation.

❤ Use "Thank You" witnessing envelopes to leave a tip when eating out or in the hotel room for the cleaning staff. They can be purchased at www. wmustore.com.

💜 Keep a small New Testament in your car, back-pack, or briefcase, to give away.

💜 Download a Bible app for your smartphone that can be used in sharing the gospel. Bible apps abound. Read all apps carefully before down-loading; some contain the plan of salvation for false religions.

CHAPTER 7

Challenges: Theirs and Ours

The four men who helped the paralytic faced quite a few obstacles before they were able to place their friend at the feet of Jesus. In any undertaking, it seems there are always challenges. Even when it comes to the fun stuff.

As a teenager I learned to water ski. No matter how hard Monday was, I knew Saturday was coming, and I could go water skiing. The day I graduated from skiing with two skis to skiing with one was one of my major skiing accomplishments. All the advice I had been given was simply to drop one ski. That did not work at all! I fell more times than I want to remember.

Since that was not working out, I decided to *start* with one ski. Surely that would be easier. I'm not so sure it was easier, but at least the falls were at a slower speed and shorter distance. With every try, my dad would ask, "Have you had enough?" Every time, my answer was, "No. Let's try again!" Then one day, it took most of the morning, but finally it happened. I was up and skiing on one ski. It was great! From that day forward, I never again skied with two skis. The falls and sore muscles were soon forgotten. There was so much more freedom with just one ski; I never wanted to give that up.

At the end of the day, my dad said, "You are the most stubborn person I have ever seen in my life!" Maybe that is why I like Peter so much; we share that common trait. It has also been the challenge of my life.

Challenges do not always come in the form of an illness, financial situation, or disability. Sometimes they come in the form of a personality trait. For me, it is being stubborn to a fault on occasion.

For me, this trait has led to moving furniture that was entirely too heavy; learning a foreign language in record time; snow skiing on the advanced slope my first day out (not a great idea!); going days without sleep to finish a project; and worst of all, putting 75 items on today's "to-do" list.

The good side of my determination is that it challenges me to try new things and do old things more efficiently and with improvement. It also has its down side. That is where the *challenge* comes into play. I have had to learn how to discern when God is calling me to put that determination to good use and, when I need, to put it down and let it go.

All of us have traits that can be either good or bad. We notice them quickly in others, but they are not so easy to see in ourselves. However, God sees and knows everything. After all, He created every inch of who we are. Psalm 139:3, 11 says, "You are familiar with *all* my ways. For you created my inmost being [emphasis added]."

What I call a challenge is what God calls His creation and His delight. Praise God that I am fearfully and wonderfully made (even in my stubbornness).

To live out active compassion, the first obstacles I have to overcome are those traits that can be good when used for good and bad when misused.

❤ Read Psalm 139.

❤ Think through your personality traits. List them with pros and cons.

❤ The psalmist says, "Your [God's] works are wonderful." You are a part of His work. List the things that are wonderful in you.

❤ Where does the psalmist say we can find God?

❤ There is no place we can go where God is not. Whatever your challenge, God is there. Praise Him for His presence with you then—now, and always.

CHALLENGE ONE: DECIDING

The paralytic's friends had to *decide* early on that they would keep their commitment to active compassion. Paul gives us an illustration in 1 Corinthians 9:24–27 of a runner in a race. The practices of a good runner are no different today than they were when Paul wrote these words. The principles used by the runner are the same principles that will help us go decide to commit in our spiritual race.

First of all, the runner has to decide to participate in the race. That may seem simple, but it is the foundation of everything else the runner does. It is this decision that will determine training schedule, diet, rest, and even the kind of shoes to wear. As a believer, the first decision is to decide to participate in the race. We could live out our lives attending church on Sunday and going to a small group or Bible study, and all of that would be a good thing. But running in the race is much more. Running the race is deciding *to invest in the lives of others*. It is deciding to show the same compassion to the lost that Paul lived out in his ministry. It is living out active compassion.

Once you decide to participate, then there is the second principle: training. Not just any kind of training, but training to win. As believers, our training comes in the form of praying and learning to hear God's voice, listening to His prompting as opportunities to minister. That is exactly what Philip did when the Spirit told him to go and talk to the Ethiopian eunuch (Acts 8:26–40). Through their conversation, Philip was able to tell him the good news of Jesus and even to baptize him before the day was over.

Training is learning God's Word and committing it to memory. When Jesus had His standoff with Satan, He won the debate through Scripture (Matthew 4:1–11). That is how we are to battle temptation. It is also the best advice to give when asked, "What should I do about . . .?" The training, along with a little determination, helps us to go the distance.

Please do not misunderstand. It is only through the power of Christ and the Holy Spirit in our lives that we can minister effectively at all. However, we all face challenges and temptations along the way, and we are the ones to determine what our response will be. We determine our yes and our no. We determine to invest in the life of another—or not to invest. We determine if we will stay with them part of the way and then leave, or if we will keep our commitment. These four men determined that they would invest in the life of the paralytic and keep that commitment.

Any good trainer will tell his runner to visualize crossing the finish line, visualize winning the medal, and visualize running the distance. Last but not least important is *focus*. Block out everything else and focus solely on the line. For us, the line is Jesus Christ. He is deserving of our total focus. Total focus on Him will transform everything else that we do. Focus is so important that Paul gives warning about it in Galatians 5:7–8: "You were running a good race. Who cut in on you to keep you from obeying the truth? That kind of persuasion does not come from the one who calls you." For us, it most often is not a matter of who cut in but what cut in: Was it business? fatigue? a person? an addiction? Our focus on Jesus will help us keep those things from cutting in on our race! Talk to Him many times each day, memorize Scripture, listen for His voice, and keep Him in focus.

I imagine the four men who helped the paralytic kept the thought of the healing power of Jesus before them through the entire event. All of their thoughts were on getting to the finish line—the feet of Jesus. Imagine the excitement and anticipation that they were feeling. Imagine the conversation between them: *The paralytic has a chance to be healed; he might actually walk!* This could have been the grandest event ever in their lives. For these men, they got to see the results of their efforts that day. We may not always see the results of our efforts but, imagine the faces that could be in heaven through your determination to finish the race!

❤ Read Galatians 6:9. Commit it to memory so that you have a reference for not growing weary.

❤ If you pray for missionaries or people groups, you are investing in lives. The people who prayed for us and our people group, for every person that came to know Christ while we were missionaries, were a part of that decision. Those people will be some of the faces my prayer warriors will see in heaven, because they decided to invest in them through prayer. Take some time today to pray for missionaries and the lives they are touching.

❤ What are the things in your life that sometimes cut in on your race? List them honestly.

❤ Now read 1 John 5:4, "For everyone born of God overcomes the world. This is the victory that has overcome the world, even our faith. Who is it that overcomes the world? Only he who believes that Jesus is the Son of God." Say a prayer of thanksgiving that we already have what it takes to run the race and get the prize: Jesus.

CHALLENGE TWO: CARRYING THE WEIGHT

The passage in the Book of Mark does not give us the details of the paralytic, such as his hair color, eye color, or weight. But we can guess that his weight was at least 130 to 150 pounds. Even for a few city blocks, that would be a heavy weight to carry.

Coming home from the Philippines on a stretcher after my back injury taught me a lot. Ever wondered where they put a stretcher in an airplane? Just behind business class. It takes up three rows, and yes, we paid for all nine seats. The paramedics rolled me to the door of the plane, and then came the scary part. The two men lifted me and my stretcher up over their head in order to get down the narrow aisles. Once we passed through the first class section, I was to be placed on the stretcher mount and fastened in.

The process only took five to ten minutes, but they were very frightening minutes. I had visions of falling off the stretcher or being dropped. Even though I was not overly heavy, you can be sure I was wishing I were even lighter! When I think about the paralytic being carried across town, I have an understanding of some of what he went through.

Most of us will not be carrying someone on a stretcher for long distances literally. But each of us have heavy weights that we carry. It is on the list of challenges we face every day. Our weights may come more in the form of children, ball practice, piano practice, bill paying, two jobs, balancing the checkbook, and all the rest. It's that list of things that make us tired and wonder how we could possibly add one more thing or person to what is already our "stretcher."

There was a time that King David's son Solomon had that feeling of too much weight. Solomon was going to build the temple that David had so hoped to build. Solomon felt overwhelmed. All the specific measurements, materials, the placing of the Ark of the Covenant, the years of labor, and keeping charge of the country felt like more than he could carry.

This is the advice David gave to Solomon: "Be strong and courageous, and do the work. Do not be afraid or discouraged, for the LORD, my God, is with you. He will not fail you or forsake you until all the work for the service of the temple of the LORD is finished" (1 Chronicles 28:20). Of course, the temple Solomon was building was a physical temple. As modern-day followers of Jesus we are building a temple as well. The temple is the church, the bride of Christ. The responsibility can seem weighty, but we can heed the words of David; we can be strong and courageous because God will be with us.

When the temple was finally completed, Solomon had the priests bring in the ark of the covenant of the Lord. For the Israelites, the ark was a symbol of the presence of God. Until the ark was in place in the temple, God's presence would not be there. The ark was heavy and cumbersome. Those who were charged with carrying the ark often walked for long hours, keeping the ark perfectly level and straight. The weight of it did not matter; what mattered was that it was carried safely to its destination.

When the ark of the covenant was placed in the temple, the priests left the Holy Place. And they began singing and praising God saying, "He is good;

his love endures forever" (2 Chronicles 5:13). Then the writer of Second Chronicles tells us that the temple was filled with a cloud and the glory of the Lord filled the temple of God.

Today, we do not carry the ark of the covenant into the church for the presence of God to be there, but I do believe, for every person we "carry" into the "temple/church," the presence of God is magnified. Every person we carry may join in the praise chorus, "He is good; his love endures forever." And then the glory of the Lord fills the new temple of God, the fellowship of believers.

💜 Read 1 Chronicles 28.

💜 What were the details of the temple?

💜 Can you understand why Solomon was overwhelmed?

💜 What is overwhelming you today? Memorize 1 Chronicles 28:20. When you feel overwhelmed remember, "He will not fail you or forsake you."

💜 Read 2 Chronicles 5.

💜 Carrying the ark of the covenant into the Temple was quite an undertaking. On occasion, convincing a friend to step into the modern-day church can be quite an undertaking as well. That is what active compassion is all about. In the end, His temple will be filled with the glory of the Lord.

Challenges: Theirs and Ours   127

CHALLENGE THREE: THE PEOPLE

The next challenge the men who helped the paralytic faced was the large crowd of people that blocked the entrance into the house. They decided to keep their commitment, carried the paralytic, and then they were faced with other people.

As a young missionary, I wanted to do something special for our national pastors. It was Christmastime, and I thought a party would be just the thing. We were expecting 125 to 150 people. Our house was not big enough for that large of a crowd but our yard was quite large and cold weather is not an issue in the tropics. For weeks before Christmas we bought food to cook as well as food to put in small baskets for each family as a gift. All of us were excited and looking forward to our first special event.

There was just one thing we did not plan on— because of the distance, many people had to travel, they came the day before. More than 100 people showed up the day before the party expecting to sleep in at our house! We had purchased a lot of food but not enough for supper, breakfast, and then Christmas lunch.

That night there were wall-to-wall people sleeping on every square-inch of floor in the house along with a large group of men and boys sleeping in the yard. Morning came and so did more guests!

The party was great fun. Our guests enjoyed the food, the games, the Christmas carols, the devotion, and the gift baskets. My boys had a great time playing Santa Claus by helping with the distribution of gifts. Soon everyone would be going home...or not.

The party lasted so long that no one was able to go home. Remember, they had to walk, and it is not safe to walk in the dark. Once again we had a house and yard full of people!

And then, the electricity went out! There is nothing like a house full of guests and no power. I was getting close to a meltdown. All I could think about were the M&M's that our friend Chellie had sent us for Christmas, but I sure did not want to share them with 140 guests.

Crowds of people can be a challenge! Jesus faced them on a regular basis. I had a large group of people for three days, He had a crowd almost all the time. In Matthew 14:13–21, we read about Jesus feeding thousands. He did not start off His day wanting to be with 5,000 people. He had just gotten word about the death of John the Baptist. He wanted to be alone. I'm sure He was sad and needed some time to mourn. He got into a small boat to withdraw for a while. Before He could get to His destination, the people heard He was coming. When He arrived, they were waiting.

At least for a few moments, He must have been discouraged and frustrated. He wanted to grieve the loss of His friend, and now that time was taken away. But read what He did: "When Jesus landed and saw a large crowd, he had compassion on them and healed their sick" (Matthew 14:14). If He'd had M&M's, He probably would have shared them.

The crowd was a challenge, but that did not stop Him from having compassion and taking care of those with needs. Challenges are just a part of the world we live in. We are always going to need to face challenges. However, we cannot allow the challenges to overshadow the need for compassion. As a matter of fact, challenges are all the more reason to have compassion; compassion for believers and nonbelievers alike who are facing their own challenges.

Active compassion is about sharing burdens, concern, and offering hope to others, regardless of our own circumstances. It was OK for me to keep my M&Ms for myself that night and enjoy them later with my husband and children. But it is never OK for me to keep Jesus and His compassion hidden from someone in need. "Carry each other's burdens, and in this way you will fulfill the law of Christ" (Galatians 6:2).

💜 Take a few minutes to read through the miracles of Jesus in the Book of Mark. What obstacles did He face? How did He overcome them?

💜 What does the attitude of Jesus teach us about being inconvenienced by one person or by a crowd?

REFLECTIONS

The day started like this: my son's car was stolen; I was late for work; and I had left my laptop at home. All before lunch! The 25 things on my "to-do" list were not even close to finished, and they all had a deadline of 5:00. We would all like to skip those kinds of days!

Sometimes it's not the day but the schedule—multiple events, deadlines, and assignments coming within a few days.

Worry and stress in our lives is not intended to take us down but rather to provide an opportunity for God's presence to shine. The Bible is full of verses on the topic. One of my favorites is 2 Kings 3:18: "This is an easy thing in the eyes of the LORD."

These words were spoken by an angel giving instructions to Elisha. The kings of Israel, Judah, and Edom had been marching with their armies for seven days. The water supply was completely gone. Stress and frustration were at a peak. If they didn't die first, how could they face the Moabites dehydrated? The king of Israel began to question God and His plan. Sound familiar? I know in the midst of my bad days and stressful schedules I get frustrated and even sometimes question God's planning. After all, He led me to serve...well, you know the conversation. But somewhere in the midst of it all, instead of blaming God, we begin looking for His help. That is just what happened with the three kings. In desperation they began looking for a prophet. This is where Elisha comes into the story.

Elisha questions their request until he hears, "It was the Lord who called us three kings together" (Kings 3:13). Elisha knew, if God was in this, He was willing to do his part. That is all God requires of us; if the Lord calls, I will do my part and trust God to do His. In the case of Elisha, God came through big!

Elisha was instructed to fill the valley with ditches, and God would fill the ditches with water. This one plan would solve *all* the problems. Not only would they have water, but also God would use the ditches to lure the Moabites into the hands of these three kings for an unquestionable victory.

Elisha followed God's instructions and the ditches were built. No doubt there had to be a little confusion in regards to the plan. The ditches would be filled with water, but that would conquer the Moabites how? God's plan may not always make sense to us, but it is always the one that works.

The next morning, the ditches were full of water flowing from the direction of Edom. What kept the Moabites from getting the water? When the Moabites saw the water, it appeared to be blood. The Moabites assumed the three kings had fought against themselves and killed one another. Thinking they could walk into the Israelite camp and take the plunder, they began their journey to the camp. What a surprise it must have been to arrive at camp and find the Israelite army waiting! The loss was so severe that the king of Moab was willing to sacrifice his own son. And God's most unusual plan did indeed solve *all* the problems!

Imagine the stress this group started with; they had no water, and they knew there was a mighty army coming their way. I would have been writing my will. But remember the words in 2 Kings 3:18: "This is an easy thing in the eyes of the Lord." No matter how bad the day, no matter how stressful the schedule, no matter how difficult the job—for the Lord it is all possible when He is directing.

I have hanging on the bulletin board in my office the words from 2 Kings 3:18 to remind me that, in the midst of a bad day, I've seen God work in miraculous ways. When I think I can't finish the list, God finishes it early. Active compassion can still be a part of my day when God is involved. It may be hard for me, but not for God!

ACTS OF COMPASSION

Be strong and courageous, do the work of the church—in the eyes of the Lord it is doable! Our only real obstacle is time. It is amazing how God can stop the clock when we have a willing spirit.

💜 Adopt a military family in your community. Pray for them, provide gift certificates for them, offer to pay for an overseas phone call for the family, offer free babysitting. Our military families give up much for our safety—share with them what "the family of God" is all about.

💜 Volunteer to host a weekly or monthly worship service at the local nursing home. Many of the residents are not able to leave the facility but can come to the dining hall to attend a time of worship. Choose music that speaks to their generation and allow for a time of sharing. We can learn much from our elders.

💜 Have a sock-hop party with music, games, and root beer floats. The cost? A package of socks. Send the socks to a children's home. Imagine trying to keep 20 or more children in socks!

💜 A food pantry is a wonderful ministry, but sometimes the food never gets used. Consider taking the food out to the community into multiple family housing projects or package it in such a way that it can be taken home by a student who may not have food for the weekend. Contact your local school for information about this program.

❤ Set up a hospital visitation ministry. Many hospitals are without a chaplain or the chaplain may be overwhelmed with the number of patients. Set up a volunteer calendar to ensure that someone is visiting hospital patients multiple times a week. Ask the local chaplain for a list of patients who may need a visitor.

CHAPTER 8

Recognizing Opportunities

The four men who carried the paralytic to Jesus perceived the opportunity to share active compassion. We don't know what the men would rather have done that day. Perhaps they were going to the market to buy or sell goods. Maybe they were going to a building site in the city. Maybe they were in the midst of family errands. Even though we do not know the specifics of their day, we can be sure that they would not have been spending the day watching television. Somehow, in the midst of their day, they heard that Jesus was in town. They had heard about the power Jesus had to heal. They knew they had an opportunity to help someone. So they acted on the opportunity in order to get the paralytic and take him to Jesus.

Just imagine what this journey must have been like. It was probably hot. The roads would have been very dusty. The exertion would have brought sweat, fatigue, and sore muscles. The dust of their feet, hands, and face would have been like mud. Their hair and beards might have been wet through and through. Their once-dry clothes would have been wet from perspiration. Most likely their hearts would have been pounding and their breath labored by the time they arrived at the house.

As they walked, what was their conversation? Did they tell the paralytic the stories of Jesus? Did they complain about the heat and the long walk through town? Was there laughter? We can only imagine all the details. What we know is that they did indeed arrive at the house where Jesus was ministering.

Whatever changes had already been made to their day, they now had a few more to come. Just when they thought their job was finished, they saw the crowd and realized their job was far from over. The crowd was so large, the men could not get their friend into the house. The original plan of taking him through the door was going to need to be adjusted if they were to finish their task.

Day-to-day life almost always brings with it a few minor adjustments. Let's call them *opportunities*. A young mother may plan to bake cookies in the afternoon, but a sick child will present a different opportunity to show caring. Something as simple as stopping by the store after work may change if traffic is unusually heavy. Most day-to-day *opportunities* are just minor annoyances.

Occasionally, though, we have to make major shifts because of the diagnosis of serious illness, the loss of a job, or the death of a loved one. These are much harder to make and have the potential to change life as we know it.

And then, there are the opportunities that come because of active compassion. Changing our schedule to help a friend in crisis or adjusting our vacation plans to volunteer in a place of need has the potential to impact eternity!

FROM ORDINARY TO EXTRAORDINARY

Gideon learned about adjusting when God spoke to him about the Midianites. Take a moment and read about Gideon in Judges 6–8.

The Israelites were in a mess. Because of their disobedience, they had been given into the hands of the Midianites for seven years. Things were so bad that the Israelites were living in caves. Just like we do today, when life was at the bottom they called on God.

For years they had been worshipping the false gods of the day. For them, it was the god of the Amorites. For us, it is the gods of America. We could spare ourselves years of living in fear and all sorts of captivities (materialism, laziness, etc.) by learning from the Israelites.

This is where Gideon came into the picture. He was hiding in a winepress, threshing his wheat when the angel came to him and said, "The LORD is with you, mighty warrior" (Judges 6:12). Gideon was far from a mighty warrior at this point; he was hiding in fear. But God saw in Gideon the potential to go from cowardly to courageous. While you may not see the great potential in yourself, God does. He sees you as His mighty warrior.

The next part of the conversation is timeless. Gideon told God all the reasons why he was not qualified to lead the Israelites in battle against the Midianites. He told his Visitor that his family was the weakest of all Israelites, and that he was the wimp in his family. Surely the wimp in the wimpiest family did not have a chance against the Midianites. Does his argument sound familiar? Has God ever called you to an opportunity to do something and your response has been to spout out all the reasons why you cannot do the job? My guess is, we would all answer yes to that question.

God's response was, "I will be with you." No matter what shifts God is asking us to make in our life in order for His work to be done, He will be with us. Not only will He be with us, He will accomplish the extraordinary work that would be impossible for us to do ordinarily.

Gideon still was not sure, so he asked God for a sign. If you have ever wondered about the patience of God, this is where you can find your answer. God was patient and gave Gideon a sign. God is always willing to answer our doubts. He never wants us to question who is in charge; He will give us what we need to know to assure us that He is in charge.

Finally Gideon was convinced. The next part of the story is important. He did everything God asked him to do in order to restore God's place in the kingdom. He tore down the altar to Baal, cut down the Asherah pole, and built a proper altar to the Lord. His actions did not come without a price. The next day, many people were upset because of what he had done. So much so that they asked for his death.

Taking a stand rarely comes without a cost. If we are to have active compassion for our country, it is time to take a stand and tear down the false altars and return in their place a proper altar for the one true God! That is a guarantee to take us from ordinary to extraordinary.

Once again, Gideon asked for confirmation from God. He put out a wool fleece—not just once but twice. He asked for the fleece to be wet and then the ground to be dry, and the ground to be wet and the fleece to be dry. God honored his request. Again, God was giving Gideon the encouragement he needed to keep going. Are you concerned about living a life of active compassion? Don't be; God will encourage you all the way as many times as you need.

Finally, Gideon began his journey to face the Midianites. His first task was putting together an army. Here was the first major adjustment. He started with 32,000 men, but God called for shifts. Gideon was left with an army of 10,000 men; however, God called for adjustments again. This time, Gideon was left with 300 men to fight powerful people of his day. Scripture says the camels alone were so many, it would have been like trying to count the sand on the beach to count them all. God wanted Gideon to fight the men that rode all those camels with only 300 men.

God is big and all-powerful; He does not need a giant army to win the battle. He only needs a few people who are committed to Him. Today, the number of people who are lost without Christ would be harder to count than the grains of sand on the beach. But God loves each and every one of them so much that He sent Jesus to die for them. He has put together His army to help Him spread the Word, His army of believers. We may be few in the scheme of things, but we serve a powerful God. With Him we can take our ordinary lives and turn them into extraordinary lives. We simply need to recognize the opportunities and make the shifts that He considers necessary, to our priorities, our finances, our attitudes, and our desires to become His.

Active compassion is about shifting from ordinary to extraordinary! Perhaps God is asking you to make some shifts in your life. Maybe it is time to look at the daily priority list, or the yearly priority list, and shift. Maybe it is time to shift vacation time to include a portion of it for missions (Remember God only needs a little to do a lot!). Maybe it is time to shift your attitude towards a family member or co-worker. When we recognize all the opportunities that God provides, and make the right shifts, then others can see Christ who compels us to active compassion.

❤ Read Ephesians 4:22–24.

❤ What shifts do you need to make based on this passage?

❤ Read 1 Corinthians 9:24–27 and Philippians 3:12–21.

In both of these passages Paul makes reference to setting a goal and running for the prize. A part of running toward the prize is setting the right priorities.

We all have 168 hours in a week. Why do some achieve more than others in those hours? Achievers determine in advance what they want to do, and then tackle the tasks in priority order. Some goals can be set for months; some goals are ever changing, and some goals are spur of the moment. The key is clearly understanding the priority. Then we have opportunities for acts of active compassion.

Make a priority list. What are the things you value the most? For the next few days, keep a list of how you spend your 168 hours. How many do you spend sleeping (which is vitally important)? How many hours do you use up by watching television? How many hours to you spend reading and studying the Bible? How many hours are you at work? How much time do you spend with friends? Family? Shopping? Now determine if your actions match your priority list. Do you need to make changes?

ONE WAY OR ANOTHER

Soon after arriving at the house, the four friends of the paralytic began working. The goal was to get the paralytic to Jesus. If one way was not a possibility, then it was time to move on to another. Mark 2:4 describes it like this, "Since they could not get him to Jesus because of the crowd, they made an opening in the roof above Jesus and, after digging through it, lowered the mat the paralyzed man was lying on." Imagine the details of this! The men had already spent the day carrying the paralytic to the house. Now they were going to have to lift him up to the roof. Remember, these were the days before automatic cranes and hydraulic lifts. They were lifting this man manually to the top of the roof. Once on the roof, they had to make an opening large enough to fit a human body through. Next would come the chore of lowering him *safely* to the floor. The men did not quit, or decide they could not do anything more, or think they had done enough already. Instead, they stayed focused on their task and looked for a way to act.

Who is to say which way is best? A group of volunteers were prayerwalking in a Muslim country in Southeast Asia. They had a daily schedule of locations and things to pray. On one particular day, they took the wrong transportation system and found themselves in a different location than the one originally scheduled for the day. Their first thoughts were to start over and try to get where they should have been. Realizing time was a factor, they chose to prayerwalk the location where they were. They divided into pairs and walked along the beach, praying for the people, businesses, and fishermen they passed as they walked. One group noticed a man who looked interested in their activities. They offered him a copy of the New Testament in his local dialect. He accepted the gift and they went on their way.

One year later, the group returned to this location. A man ran up to them, asking if they were the same group that had been there a year before. He wanted to know if they recalled the book he was given. As they began talking to this man, they learned that he had taken the New Testament home and read through the entire book. Because of reading this copy of the Bible, he accepted Jesus as his

Savior. Hebrews 4:12 is still true today: "For the word of God is living and active. Sharper than any double-edged sword, it penetrates even to dividing soul and spirit, joints and marrow; it judges the thoughts and attitudes of the heart." Not only had he met Jesus because of this book, he had shared the book with others, and they too now knew Jesus as their Savior. The group had grown to 250, and they were looking for someone who could help them know what to do next. All they knew was to meet regularly and read the book together. God took care of the rest.

💜 Take time out now to read Genesis 37–50—the story of Joseph.

Joseph had a dream from God that he would one day be ruler over his family. Before seeing that dream come to fruition, Joseph went through many trials and course changes. He was sold into slavery, promoted to a position of leadership, accused of a wrong doing, put back into prison, and a multitude of other events. Throughout it all, Joseph stayed focused on God. He trusted that what he thought was plan A was not in alignment with God's plan A.

The day finally came when he was second in command in his country. It was during a time of drought, and his family was in serious crisis. Because of Joseph's position, he was able to restore his family and provide all that they needed. In the midst of it all, God's name was glorified through Joseph's testimony of God's grace and his act of forgiveness towards his brothers who had sold him into slavery. Wow! That is a very short version of a very long story.

What if he had given up while in slavery? What if he had lost hope when he was accused of rape? What if he had not gone on through each and every stage of the plan? The story might have had a different ending. But Joseph stayed focused and summed it up in Genesis 50:20 like this, "You intended to harm me, but God intended it for good to accomplish what is now being done, the saving of many lives." Joseph provided all the food necessary for his family. He displayed active compassion so that many would be saved.

Active compassion requires a willingness to go through as many plans as necessary to get to the goal. There is joy in completion, but more importantly there are people without Jesus who need us to keep trying until we find that one thing, that one word, that one Scripture, that one kind deed, that one event that will take them to Jesus.

I have no doubt that these four friends of the paralytic were exhausted at the end of their journey. I have no doubt that Joseph wanted to quit on more than one day. But they each stayed focused for the cause. That is what God's way is all about. It is trying again and again for the cause, bringing the lost to Christ.

❤ After reading the account of Joseph, list the things that were delays in Joseph's final destination.

❤ What were the lessons he learned during the delays that helped him later to prepare for the job of second-in-command?

💜 How did those delays ultimately lead him to his final destination?

💜 What was his greatest act of compassion? If Joseph had reached the place of leadership soon after his dream, do you think he would have been ready to show that kind of active compassion? Why?

WHATEVER IT TAKES

The four men who helped the paralytic were willing to do whatever it took to get the man to Jesus. They were willing to do heavy labor, fight crowds, and climb walls. We find that same determination throughout the New Testament in the life of Jesus, the life of the disciples, the life of Paul, and many others. What about today? Are there people willing to do whatever it takes? Are they living lives of active compassion?

The answer is yes. As a missionary I have been privileged to meet many of them. One is Harold Watson. Harold is an agriculturalist/farmer from Mississippi. He and his wife, Joyce, were called to the Philippines in the 1960s. Harold realized the farmers in the Philippines were on their way to complete devastation and starvation if they continued to use the traditional farming methods. Growing crops on the side of a mountain with no modern tools or equipment is not an easy task. As Americans, our first thought is to buy the equipment and give it to the farmers; however, Harold knew that was not the answer. What happened when the equipment broke? Where would the money come from for the fuel? Harold often said, "It is better to teach a man to fish than to give him a fish."

Harold (who was echoing many others) started with the first way, develop a better method of farming than "slash and burn." (Slash and burn farming involves burning off the vegetation before planting. This method had been used planting season after planting season. In just a few years, the ground was depleted of all its nutrients.) It took many tries before he found all the answers. After many years of experimenting and testing, he found a method that worked—S.A.L.T. (Sloped Agricultural Land Technology). The farmer would plant hedgerows between rows of crops. The hedgerow plants returned much needed nutrients to the soil as well as prevented the soil from washing away in the tropical rains.

Not only did Harold develop a more productive way of farming, he looked for ways to bring the message of Christ into his agricultural classes. By the time Harold retired, a demonstration farm had been established that brought in thousands of Filipino farmers and dignitaries from countries all over Asia to study Harold's methods. Additionally, he received the highest award given by the Philippine government to a civilian, the Ramon Magsaysay Award.

There have been countless numbers of poor Filipino farmers who have met Christ while learning a better method of farming. Harold did not set out to be world renowned as an agriculturist or nationally recognized for the improvements he gave to farmers or the difference he made in poverty and hunger. He set out with active compassion for the hungry and to share the love of Christ with them. His active compassion was the driving force that caused him to look for ways in which poor farmers could support their families and put food on their tables. Harold was willing to do whatever it took to equip people to feed themselves. He gave more than 35 years of his life to the task. In retirement he still travels, teaches, trains, and advises agricultural leaders all over the world, and he is still looking for better ways, more efficient ways, and more productive ways to help hungry people feed themselves.

Sixteen thousand children a day die of hunger-related issues. In the Philippines, the number of deaths due to hunger have decreased because a farmer from Mississippi was willing to do whatever it takes to teach someone to grow their own food.

Active compassion is not giving up. It is a willingness to do whatever it takes to make a difference in a life, a country, the world. Active compassion took Harold to the Philippines. It took Jesus to the Cross. Where is it taking you?

❤ What is your passion?

❤ How can your passion make a difference? Remember, God uses everything—a passion for weaving, recycling, or accounting—as an avenue to lead someone to Christ. It is a matter of looking for the open door, or roof, as the case may be.

❤ Pray and ask God to show you how you can use your passion to make a difference.

Recognizing Opportunities   149

REFLECTIONS

In the movie *Amazing Grace,* Billy says to Wilbur, "We are too young to realize that certain things are impossible; so we do them anyway." Were my father still alive, he would have said, "Billy must be related to my hardheaded daughter, Gayla." In gymnastics, when I was told five-foot-seven was too tall for aerial moves, I did them anyway. What did height have to do with it? When I was learning to water ski on one ski, I was told that we needed a ski rope with split handles. We didn't have one, so I used our single-handled rope and did it anyway. What did a handle have to do with it? Looking back, I see why my dad might have thought I was hard headed.

As believers we are challenged to grow and mature in our biblical knowledge and in our relationship with the Lord. There are hundreds of Scripture passages backing up the challenge to grow. It is a lifestyle we should all embrace. But I wonder if there should also be little bit of Billy's philosophy in us too. I've looked back through Scriptures and found many people who must have followed Billy's line of thinking. Here are just a few:

> "Is anything too hard for the LORD?" (Genesis 18:14), the Lord said to Abraham. Isaac was born when Abraham was one hundred years old!

When Elisha instructed Joram to dig ditches in the valley because God was going to fill them with water in spite of a drought, Elisha assured the king, "This is an easy thing in the eyes of the LORD" (2 Kings 3:18). The next morning the waters came.

Jeremiah proclaimed, "Nothing is too hard for you" (Jeremiah 32:17). And God delivered his people from exile.

Nehemiah miraculously rebuilt the walls of Jerusalem with 50,000 of his countrymen, in 52 days, in the midst of intense opposition. Esther went against protocol and went before the king in an effort to save her people. The king heard her plea and an entire people group was spared. Mordecai's words rang true, "Who knows but that you have come to royal position for such a time as this?" (Esther 4:14).

The angel told Mary, "For nothing is impossible with God" (Luke 1:37). And a virgin gave birth to the Savior.

What if any one of these had said, "This can't be done"? Isaac would not have been born; the ditches would not have been dug; the Israelites would have remained in exile; the wall around Jerusalem would have remained in ruins; Haman would have killed the Jews; and Mary...well, many things would have been different.

Whatever you undertake for the Lord, remember Billy's philosophy, "We are too young to realize that certain things are impossible, so we do them anyway." Or maybe it is really, "For nothing is impossible with God!"

ACTS OF COMPASSION

A missional lifestyle is not just for the individual; it is also for the family. Gather in the troops, young and old alike, and head out on mission!

💜 When planning a family vacation look for ways to be on mission. It could be the vacation is a mission trip internationally or locally through Family-FEST. Or it may be that while at a theme park, ocean beach front, or lakeside park, ministry happens. Giving water to a lifeguard, singing worship songs around a campfire, talking with people while in line for the best ride—or carrying a tray for a mom at the fast-food restaurant—are all ways to minister while on vacation. Showing our families that ministry happens wherever we are whenever we are there is one way to show that Jesus really is a part of our lives everyday and works through us everyday when we take time to look around us.

💜 As a family, adopt a child at school that needs help. While your children are shopping for a new lunchbox, pencils, and other school items, purchase those same items for a child in need. The local school can provide the information you need.

- Offer to be the lawn service for an elderly family in the neighborhood.

- As a family, adopt an unreached people group. Pray for them at each meal time. Consider a mission trip to the area, or partnering with a missionary in the area. Information for unreached people groups can be found at www.imb.org.

- While studying US history, connect with a missionary serving Native Americans. Collect items, make cards, or plan a visit. Remember to pray for the Native Americans who do not yet know Christ as Savior.

CHAPTER 9

Laying Down

Eventually, the four men had to be willing to release the paralytic—lay him down and let him go. Once they lowered him through the roof, they were no longer in control. Not being in control is a scary place to be. We all like to be in control at least in some areas of our life. But on occasion, we have to lay down something for the sake of another person's salvation.

Abraham is an example of someone with this willingness to lay down. He was willing to lay down his beloved son, Isaac, if that was what God wanted him to do. Take a moment and read the story in Genesis 22.

God called out to Abraham and instructed, "Take your son, your only son, Isaac, whom you love, and go to the region of Moriah. Sacrifice him there as a burnt offering on one of the mountains I will tell you about." We can all agree that is a tough order! But Abraham followed through. How did he do it?

First of all, Abraham knew without a doubt this was coming from God. If that were the case, then God had a plan. John 10:2–5 is a New Testament reminder of the importance of recognizing the voice of God. "His sheep follow him because they know his voice. But they will never follow a stranger; in fact, they will run away from him because they do not recognize a stranger's voice" (v. 4–5).

Like sheep with their shepherd, Abraham had spent a lot of time with God and was very familiar with His call. He first heard God's call when he was 75. He and God had a conversation again when he lied in Egypt about his wife, Sarai (Genesis 12). God helped him as he dealt with Lot (Genesis 14). God made a covenant with Abraham and told him, "Do not be afraid, Abram. I am your shield, your very great reward" (Genesis 15:1). God changed Abram's name to Abraham (Genesis 17). Abraham pled with God for Sodom (Genesis 18). And then at last Isaac was born (Genesis 21).

Then, he was called to lay down this treasured son. Abraham had at least 25 years of walking with God and had learned about God's faithfulness. He knew and trusted God's character. For us to let go and let God, we have to know who God really is. Abraham knew God's character as holy, just, good, and loving. He knew God as true to His word, and God had told him he would be the father of many nations. Abraham knew that God loved Isaac. And he knew God as a God of provision.

The key was to keep listening! Imagine if Abraham had said, "OK, God," and then closed his ears. He never would have heard the angel who gave this instruction, "Do not lay a hand on the boy.... Do not do anything to him. Now I know that you fear God, because you have not withheld from me your son, your only son" (Genesis 22:12). God wants our all.

At that point, Abraham looked up and there he saw a ram. The ram became the sacrifice. Abraham called the mountain, "On the mountain of the LORD it will be provided" (Genesis 22:14). Laying down led to provision—salvation for Isaac, and eventually salvation for the world. Active compassion may call for you to lay down _____ (you fill in the blank).

💜 Read John 10.

💜 What does Jesus say the good shepherd lays down for his sheep? How did that foretell what was to come?

💜 Reread verses 27–28. Can we ever be snatched from the hand of Jesus?

💜 Take a few minutes to rejoice in that truth!

💜 Why did the Jews want to stone Jesus? Isn't it interesting that it was not for doing good but for proclaiming who He was? Do you see similarities for believers today?

♥ How does this chapter end? Do you believe that speaking the truth is enough for many to believe in Jesus today? Why or why not?

♥ How can the words in John 10 help someone know how to live a life of active compassion?

GIVING OUR LIFE

"Greater love has no one than this, that he lay down his life for his friends" (John 15:13).

Going to the dentist was one of the things I took for granted prior to going to the missions field. In the US, no matter how small the city or town, you can always find a dentist office. As a matter of fact, my best friend, Jan, is a dentist. I don't know what I would do without her both as a friend and as my dental consultant.

But in the Philippines, in our city of 350,000 people, dentist offices were not so easy to find. Once they were found, the quality of care was always in question. The precautions that dentists take in the US to prevent the spread of HIV/AIDS, hepatitis, and other diseases, were not used in the Philippines. For us, the risk was too great to take, so we only saw a dentist when we were in the US. Basically, that means that every four years we saw our dentist.

Our furloughs were spent at First Baptist Church, Conway, Arkansas. Jack Logan was a member there and also our dentist. As soon as we arrived at the mission house, we would receive a call from Jack. He would say, "It's been four years, we will have a lot of work ahead of us. When can you come in?" Over the weeks and months ahead, we would find ourselves in Jack's dental chair frequently. Not only did he want to see us our first week in the country, he wanted to see us our last week in the country as well. I guess he thought one more round of fluoride treatment might make his job easier on our next visit to Conway.

Jack would ask us, while we were sitting in his dentist chair, to tell him every detail of what God was doing in our work. I used to wonder how he expected us to talk with cotton, drills, and all the stuff in our mouths. But nonetheless, he was genuinely interested in our work. My husband would respond, "Why don't you come visit us and find out firsthand?"

Jack knew that fillings were not an option in a third-world country. Dentists pull hundreds of teeth in only a few days in countries with little to no dental care. Jack already had arthritis in his hands, and he was concerned that he would not have the hand strength to pull that many teeth. Even though he was saying no it was easy to see that God was working and one day Jack would be saying yes.

The day came when Jack did indeed say yes to a missions trip to Nicaragua. Just as he had imagined, he pulled hundreds of teeth before the week was over. But he also shared Jesus that week. And not once did he have a problem with his hands. When we saw Jack after that first trip he was beaming! It was all he could talk about, and he could not wait to return.

Jack went back to Nicaragua many times and impacted more lives than we will ever know. But without a doubt, his last trip had the greatest impact of all.

Jack arranged for a fishing boat to take a group out on Lake Nicaragua. Sadly, the boat overturned during a sudden storm. The water was cold, the waves were high, and several of the group perished—including Jack—who *chose* to lay down his life—to save the lives of two teens. Jack lived out John 15:13 that day!

There are many things to hold onto that are "safe." Age is one; I'm too old or too young. Yet one of our missions volunteers was an 82-year-old nurse who did more work than five others who were younger. A 12-year-old girl in Maryland has already led over 100 people to a relationship with Jesus Christ. Certainly either one of them could have said, "I am too old." or "I am too young."

I've seen entire families minister together, both in America and on the foreign missions field. Our boys loved to go to a refugee camp to distribute food, or to hold up the pictures for a Bible study, or to help plant trees on a farm. Our entire missions career was spent working together as a family. The Howse family, serving as North American Mission Board missionaries, served side by side at rodeos. They were willing to give their lives so that others would have a chance to meet Jesus.

Some say, "I just cannot afford to go on a missions trip." Even a friend of mine thought that until this year when she and her husband committed to go to Romania. They did not have the money when they said they would go, but they decided to let go of the excuse and trust God. By the time the money was needed, they had it all.

The list of what we hold onto is endless: education, jobs, health, and so on. Whatever it is that we are holding onto, when we give it to God, Jesus will be right there to take our hand and someone else may have the chance to grab hold of the hand of Jesus with us.

💜 Are you are holding onto what you need to give? Ask Jesus to take your hand to help you to give.

💜 How can you help someone you know meet Jesus?

💜 Read Matthew 10:39. What does it say to you?

GIVING UP

Giving up everything is not a new struggle people face today. Many people who have gone before us have faced this same decision. Many have found the courage to give up. Take, for example, Zacchaeus, the tax collector.

Tax collectors in the day of Jesus had the means to make an almost unlimited amount of income. It was a common practice for them to add a percentage of money to the top of the amount of owed taxes. Much like a "loan shark" might do today. Whatever the amount of the overage was additional income for the tax collector. Just imagine when multiplied by thousands, the amount of money that could be earned. The family of Zacchaeus was well taken care of because of these unethical practices.

When Jesus came into town, Zacchaeus was curious. Evidently, Zacchaeus was a short man because he climbed up in a tree in order to see Jesus. I have to wonder if there were not additional reasons for this action. Maybe because he would not have been liked or respected in society, he did not want to face the hissing and jeering that was sure to come his way.

As children, we learned to sing, "Zacchaeus was a wee little man, and a wee little man was he." At this point in his life, not only was he small in size but he was also small in character. He was cruel to the people in his region. He was unscrupulous in his practices. He was lacking in integrity, lacking in love, and certainly lacking in joy.

Did you notice in the story of Zacchaeus that he did not call on Jesus? Instead, Jesus called Zacchaeus. Just like He still calls our names today. Jesus knew the state of Zacchaeus's life. He knows the state of our lives today. There is nothing that is hidden from Him. Even those things that absolutely no one knows other than ourselves are known to Jesus. He knows our real weight, real dress size, and our real heart. And He still loves us, just like He still loved Zacchaeus.

Jesus was probably the only one who loved Zacchaeus at this point. People like Zacchaeus are what my husband refers to as "porcupines"—they are hard to hug but you have to love them anyway because they are God's creation. All of us know people, believers and nonbelievers, that are difficult to "hug." But you never know what might happen because of something as simple as a hug!

Jesus called up to Zacchaeus and invited Himself to the tax collector's home. Jesus continues to invite Himself into the homes of our hearts. Zacchaeus could have ignored Jesus. He could have stared off down the road. But instead, he came down from the tree rejoicing that Jesus had called.

For Zacchaeus, this was the point at which he decided to give up everything; his ability to bring home lots of extra money, his reputation, the way he had been doing his job for these many years. He decided to lay it all down and take the hand of the One who could redeem him and offer him eternal security.

In the end, Zacchaeus was blessed in abundance with the kind of blessings that last for eternity. His entire household may have received Christ that day because of his decision to answer Jesus when He called.

❤ Read the story of Zacchaeus in Luke 19:1–9.

❤ Following God is about giving up anything that may be standing between us and someone meeting Jesus. Spend some time today praying about what in your life it is time to give up and lay down.

REFLECTIONS

The parable of the lost coin in Luke 15:8–10 came alive to me just a few months after my wedding. Freddy and I were living in seminary housing at Southern Seminary. In case you have ever wondered, seminary housing does not come with a self-cleaning oven or self-defrosting refrigerator. So, periodically, I had to spend my day cleaning the oven and defrosting the refrigerator. Otherwise, baking became hazardous, and the freezer was full of ice instead of food.

One Saturday afternoon, after finishing my monthly kitchen chores, I decided to make cookies. Freddy and my seminary neighbors loved the chocolate oatmeal cookies that are cooked on top of the stove. I spooned the cookies out on aluminum foil, and all that was left was cleaning the dirty dishes. I removed my wedding rings, placed them on the foil with the cookies, and started washing dishes. Once the dishes were finished, I took a few hours to finish up homework for the weekend. By the time it was all done, the cookies were cool. I removed them from the foil, placed them in a container, wadded up the foil, and threw it away.

Yes, you guessed it, my rings were still in the foil. It was Sunday morning before I realized they were lost and Tuesday afternoon before I remembered where I had put them in our 225-square-foot apartment. Freddy and I had looked through the trash hundreds of times, but it did not occur to me to unwad the foil. Just like the parable, we called our friends and neighbors and had a celebration party! To this day, making chocolate-oatmeal cookies causes me to shiver!

For those three days, my lost wedding rings consumed my thoughts. While in class, while at work, while at the library, while at home, when going to bed, when getting up—losing my rings was all I thought about. Where could they be? How could I have lost something so precious? Would I ever find them? No other rings would ever be the same. When they were found, the entire campus knew from my shouts of joy.

My rings were valuable, but only to Freddy and me. Souls, on the other hand, are valuable to God. So much so that "while we were yet sinners Christ died for us" (Romans 5:8). The Parable of the Lost Coin ends by saying, "In the same way, I tell you, there is rejoicing in the presence of the angels of God over one sinner who repents" (Luke 15:10).

Bottom line, that is what living a life of active compassion is all about: finding the lost, showing them love, telling them about the eternal life that is available with Christ, and rejoicing with the angels in heaven when even one is found. That's a party I can be a part of!

ACTS OF COMPASSION

Human exploitation is a serious issue that effects every generation—from bullying to human trafficking. Like Zacchaeus, the tax collector, the people involved are hated by society but loved by Jesus.

💜 Volunteer with the local police department in providing education for local schools, hotels, and malls. These are all areas where traffickers seize people for the purposes of trafficking.

💜 Combat bullying by being intentional in modeling an attitude that honors Christ at the workplace, the store, or school. Avoid the gossip stations (including those at church); follow the model, "if you can't say anything nice, don't say anything at all." Above all, model biblical integrity in every aspect of your life.

💜 Be intentional in seeking opportunities to minister. Carry someone's luggage at the airport. Offer to take a grocery cart back. Pick up the trash at a local park. Buy a case of sports drink for the local high school sports program. Buy two pizzas instead of one and share the other. Give up your space in line. As you live, "look up in the trees"—there might be a Zacchaeus in need of encouragement.

♥ Volunteer to hold a "drug baby" during detox. The baby did not choose to be born addicted and needs a lot of love and care during those early days of life. The life you are holding may be a life that changes others' for the better.

CHAPTER 10

The Miracle

The paralytic's four friends had quite an adventure because of their active compassion. They noticed a man who needed help. They cared about him. They extended a helping hand. They shared Christ. They put their words into action. They decided to make a commitment. They faced challenges along the way. They recognized opportunities and made shifts. They were willing to lay down and give up. And they became a part of the miracle.

A LIFE CHANGED

The story of the paralytic is a story of a life changed, the story of a miracle. Just imagine what it must have been like for him. The man once bound by paralysis could now walk, run, skip, jump, feel the water on his feet, go to the market, perhaps fall in love, work and support himself, gather his own firewood, and he could follow Jesus. Not only did his physical life change, but his spiritual life changed as well. His eternity changed. He could go about spreading the Word and helping others change their eternal destination.

Notice in the paralytic's story, his friends did not yell down to Jesus and tell Him what to do. They just watched and learned—a theme that is repeated throughout the Bible! The disciples learned as they watched Jesus heal the sick. The Israelites learned as they watched God rescue them from captivity. We, too, get to learn as we watch the miracles around us every single day.

On the missions field, it was our privilege to see many miracles. A co-worker was poisoned while working in a Muslim village. She never even got a stomachache when normally she should have died. The entire village accepted Christ as Savior because they, too, were all amazed because they had never seen anything like this.

One of our missionaries was hijacked in his car one night while traveling back home from one of the seminaries. Three Filipino pastors were riding with him. When they were flagged at a checkpoint, they soon learned that it was not a military checkpoint, but rather a group of men looking for someone to kidnap. The four men were tied and put in the back of the van the missionary had been driving. The kidnappers could not drive a standard shift and eventually found themselves stuck in a ditch. When the missionary offered to drive, he was untied and put once again behind the steering wheel. He requested that some of them get out and push. Instead of a few, they *all* got out. When the van was finally pushed out of the ditch, the missionary didn't stay around to let the kidnappers get back in; he just kept driving all the way home—most of the way in first gear, he said! He and the other men faced an uncertain outcome, but because of the confusion created, they were set free. Was it the kidnappers' poor judgment or was it God intervening?

My husband and his team of pastors were traveling into a remote area when they were told that they should not stay overnight because of threats that had come to the village. They turned back and stopped at the closest village to stay the night. As it turned out the attack was not for the village they had planned to visit but for the village where they were staying the night. Hand grenades and automatic weapons disrupted the quiet night. My husband and his companions left their hut and ran to a cave by the river where they spent the night waiting for the first opportunity to hike out. After a long night of fighting, my husband and his friends emerged from their refuge without a single scratch.

Chinese Baptist Church in Davao City made the decision to make prayer a priority. Every Friday night there are as many as 500 people gathered together to pray. The prayers are not in the form of a "to-do" list for God, but the form of proclaiming, "Your will be done." The church is not air-conditioned nor is it large enough for 500 people. The windows are opened and chairs placed outside around the parameter of the building. People who can't find a seat inside, sit outside, and because the windows are open, they too can participate in the prayer service. At the end of the service, an offering is taken for missions. The leadership team then prays for the right place to send the monies received. The collection is given to a missions cause within the week.

On one particular week, the people felt led to give the money to one of the US missionaries. When the missionary was given the money, he said that he had no need for it at that time and suggested that maybe it should go to someone else. But the pastor was sure he had heard God correctly and told the missionary to keep the money and wait for the right time for it to be used. Little did the missionary know the right time would come the very next day.

The missionary traveled to a training project where he talked with a man who had brought his entire group to the training center. They thought they had raised enough money for the trip, but they had not. For days they had been sleeping outside and eating fruit from the trees for their meals. The group had prayed as to what they should do and felt led to continue on at the training center; their need would be met.

The missionary asked how much money they needed to pay for their lodging. And, yes, it was the exact amount that had been given to him by the pastor. The miracle, God connecting the dots. The group received the training, returned home to begin new Bible studies, and have sent two more groups for training.

And then, there is the miracle of A and KP. The two men had been enemies most of their adult lives. One a Muslim, one not. Both very violent members of vigilante groups. Both had been a part of killing each other's family members and robbing each other's people groups.

While A was out on a raid, he noticed a young woman who was more beautiful than any other. He demanded from her family that she be given to him as his wife. When you are carrying an M16 rifle your demands are typically met. The young woman, a follower of Jesus, asked permission to take her Bible. Every day, she read her Bible and prayed for her husband. Several months later, A was not able to sleep. He did not sleep for several nights. Blaming his ailments on the Bible, he decided it needed to be thrown out. He rummaged through the house until he found the Bible. Before he destroyed it, he decided to read it and try to learn why it had such power that it could keep him from sleep. As he read the words, he began to realize what was missing in his own life, a relationship with Jesus. He is now a follower of Jesus.

KP also married a Christian woman. It was through her influence that he too came to know the Lord. His life was once full of anger, but when he received Christ, the anger was completely gone.

These two men attended a gathering of believers. Former enemies, who in the past would have killed one another, were at the same place at the same time. The other believers, knowing the reputation of the men, were concerned how this meeting might turn out. A and KP asked for time on the platform. That night, they publicly asked forgiveness for one another, cried, embraced, and prayed for one another. It was a miracle of gigantic proportions. The people had never seen anything like it. From that night forward, the number of unreached people groups coming to know the Lord has multiplied tenfold.

God is still using miracles to bring glory to His name. Not all are as dramatic as being saved from poison, eluding bandits, or escaping hand grenade and gun fire, but all have the same dramatic results: lives changed for eternity.

THE MIRACLE OF ETERNAL LIFE…JESUS

God has been a God of miracles since the beginning of time. It started with creation. But Adam and Eve abused the resources they had. It was that abuse of their resources that separated them from God. What had been a perfect ongoing life was now a sinful limited life. But God had another plan.

"*But God…*" The wages of sin is death, so when Adam and Eve sinned, they should have died, *but God* chose another plan. When the people of the world turned their back on God, Noah should have drowned in the flood, *but God* gave him the ark because he was a man who walked with God. When Israel was in need of a king, David was a simple shepherd, *but God* made him the shepherd of His chosen people. The paralytic at the gate should never have walked, *but God* healed his legs. When the world needed a Savior, Jesus could have stayed with God, *but God* sent Him to earth to die on the Cross for our sins that we might have the chance to join them in heaven.

Prior to Jesus, salvation came through faith by receiving what God had revealed. The laws became tedious over time. What could and could not be done on the Sabbath was always a debate. Taking care to sacrifice animals and minding every rule was a challenge. How could one be sure the animal was flawless? How could people know if they had done everything exactly right?

It was impossible for humans to get it all right. God desired more than anything for the men and women He created to join Him for eternity. So the decision was made to provide the greatest miracle of all: Jesus. He left His place on the right hand of His Father in heaven and was born of a virgin. He lived a flawless life with no sin (inwardly or outwardly). He was in perfect unity with God. Then the day came that He would become the ultimate sacrifice for the sin of everyone ever born or yet to be born. The complete and total payment for humankind's sin. You only need to believe that Jesus is the way and the truth and the life. No one comes to the Father except by Him. If you believe in Him as Savior, no other sacrifice will ever be needed. No other law will ever be required. No good deeds list will be required. He made the impossible—sinful people entering into heaven—possible by paying the price.

WHO WILL BE NEXT?

Here is our responsibility. Who will we take to the feet of Jesus? What miracle will we watch? When will we hear, "they were all amazed because they had never seen anything like this"?

REFLECTIONS

In Luke 19, we read about Jesus' triumphal entry into the city of Jerusalem. The crowd of disciples praised God in loud voices, and the Pharisees in the crowd became annoyed. They yelled out, "Teacher, rebuke your disciples!"

Today, we may not have annoyed Pharisees in our midst but there are certainly others all around us who say: "I don't want to hear about Jesus." "Don't talk about church at work." "I want to be your friend but don't talk to me about Jesus."

Jesus says to the Pharisees, "I tell you…if they [my disciples] keep quiet, the stones will cry out" (Luke 19:40). God will make Himself known—if not through the praises of His people, then through the earth He created. In recent history, Jesus' declaration has been proven to be true.

In 2004, the world watched in awe the results of a 9.1 magnitude tsunami that hit countries along the Indian Ocean, including Thailand, a country where Buddhism prevails. For many months following the tsunami, believers from all over America went to Thailand to help in the midst of the devastation. One of those volunteers was a former missionary to Thailand. He asked a Thai pastor, "Has the trauma of the tsunami hurt your efforts to tell others about God?" The Thai pastor answered, "No! It has helped me. I have been telling my neighbors about the power of God and showing them in the Bible how God is all-powerful. Now I have proof. He showed His power in the tsunami."

In 2010, a magnitude 7 earthquake hit Haiti, a country where over half the population practices voodoo. Only weeks later, a massive earthquake ripped through Chile, where Catholicism prevails.

As believers, we have the opportunity to shout out His praises every day in multiple ways. We can share our praises of thanksgiving with family and friends. We can praise God when we tell our testimony. And we can praise Him when we read a passage of Scripture to someone who needs encouragement.

We can also praise Him with our attitude, actions, and reactions. When we react in kindness instead of anger, live with integrity, or work above and beyond the call of duty, we give praise to God.

We also shout His praises when we serve others. Whether it be on a local or foreign missions trip, by taking food to a neighbor, or by serving at a clothes closet for the homeless, we sing God's praises to those we serve.

Jesus said that if His people keep quiet, that "the *stones* will cry out" (Luke 19:40; emphasis added). Jesus died for me and *I* want to be the one to shout it out—through my testimony and through living a life of *active* compassion.

ACTS OF COMPASSION

On this journey of life, shout out God's praises by living out active compassion. In the Great Commission we read, "Go ye therefore..." (Matthew 28:20 KJV). Translated literally, this full verse means, "As you go, make disciples."

- ❤ As you go to the doctor's or dentist's office for your yearly check up, take Christian literature that can be left in the waiting room.

- ❤ As you go to the pharmacy, offer to pick up and deliver meds to the sick and shut-in.

- ❤ As you carry the trashcan to the end of the driveway, take your neighbor's as well.

- ❤ As you buy a coffee, buy one for a server to enjoy.

- ❤ As you buy Christmas/birthday gifts, buy one for someone in need.

- ❤ As you go to church, bring guests with you.

- ❤ As you travel, engage in spiritual conversations.

- ❤ As you pay the cashier, say a word of kindness.

❤ As you work, work with the attitude of Christ.

❤ As you pray, pray for the world.

❤ As you go...take Christ with you! He will lead the way to the lost.

Active Compassion Journal

Active Compassion Journal

Active Compassion Journal

Active Compassion Journal

Active Compassion Journal

Active Compassion Journal

Active Compassion Journal

Active Compassion Journal

Active Compassion Journal

_____

_____

_____

_____

_____

_____

_____

_____

_____

_____

_____

_____

_____

_____

_____

_____

Active Compassion Journal

New Hope® Publishers is a division of WMU®, an international organization that challenges Christian believers to understand and be radically involved in God's mission. For more information about WMU, go to www.wmu.com. More information about New Hope books may be found at www.newhopedigital.com. New Hope books may be purchased at your local bookstore.

Use the QR reader on your
smartphone to visit us online at
www.newhopedigital.com

If you've been blessed by this book,
we would like to hear your story.
The publisher and author welcome your comments and
suggestions at: newhopereader@wmu.org.

Additional Titles from New Hope:

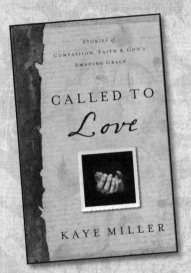

Called to Love:
Stories of Compassion, Faith, and God's Amazing Grace
Kaye Miller
ISBN-13: 978-1-59669-235-0 • $14.99

Compelled by Love:
The Most Excellent Way to Missional Living
Ed Stetzer and Philip Nation
ISBN-13: 978-1-59669-227-5 • $14.99

Available in bookstores everywhere

For information about these books or any New Hope product, visit www.newhopedigital.com.